RAY BENTLEY

the passion, wisdom

and redemption of King Solomon

GOD'S
PURSUING
LOVE

ACKNOWLEDGEMENTS

I would like to give special thanks to Jennie Gillespie for her tremendous help in writing this book. Her research, insights, and talent helped to bring this story to life. Also, special thanks to her husband, Bob Gillespie, for his vision to bring this story to fruition. Lastly, I would like to thank Neil Godding for his cover design, Romy Godding (most excellent proofreader), Lance Emma, Sarah Yardley, and the rest of the Calvary Distribution team for their publishing skills and their hearts for ministry.

§

Most of all, thank you to my "Shulamite," my wife Vicki, the love of my life and the one who has taught me more about love than I could have ever dreamed.

CONTENTS

THE SHEPHERD GIRL AND THE KING

Make haste, my beloved, and be like a gazelle or a young stag on the mountains of spices.

—Song 8:14

ONCE upon a time, in the north country of ancient Israel, a king named Solomon owned a vineyard. Situated in the mountain district of Ephraim, the land was rented out to a struggling family.

Sadly, the husband died, leaving his wife and young children to struggle on their own. Two brothers and two sisters—one girl still quite young—were left to work the vineyard. In assuming the burdens of their father's role, the brothers grew harsh and full of anger. Frustrated, they turned their bitterness toward their youngest sister, the Shulamite girl. She bore the brunt of their resentment.

Her brothers pushed all the hardest farm tasks onto her. They denied her privileges and the respect young girls expect, growing up in a Hebrew household. Daily, she watered, pruned, and set traps for the foxes that spoiled the vines. She protected and tended the family flock of sheep, always searching out adequate pastures. She worked hard from sunrise to the end of the day.

My own vineyard I have not kept, she sighed one day to herself. While her sheep were drinking from a woodland spring, she leaned over to peer at her reflection. *I am dark, but still lovely.* She wasn't like the other daughters of Jerusalem, the wealthy young girls with time and means to pamper themselves. As she worked out in the fields, wondering what would become of her life, she often watched them, laughing and talking as they walked down the roads, carrying themselves with beauty and grace and adorned in the finest clothes.

One spring day, while tending her flocks, she was startled to hear someone approaching from behind. Turning, she saw a very tall and handsome stranger watching her. He had come to water his own flock at the same spring.

Who is this stranger? she wondered. She knew all the local shepherds and would have remembered him. A flush rushed to her face before she could compose herself. She smiled cautiously, then met his intense gaze for several seconds. An inexplicable sense of joy swept over her. Then, just as quickly as the sun had broken over her soul, a cloud darkened her countenance. She turned her eyes down and spoke softly, "Do not look upon me, because I am dark, because the sun has tanned me. My mother's sons were angry with me; they made me the keeper of the vineyards, but my own vineyard I have not kept."

She felt unlovely and unworthy.

Slowly, he drew near, and with a gentle hand, lifted her face until her eyes met his and said, "Behold, you are fair, my love! Behold, you are fair!"

At that moment, a deep friendship began. As spring blossomed, their affection grew into love. With love came mutual expressions of joy and ardor. "You are handsome, my beloved!" the Shulamite responded to his loving words.

Then one day, the shepherd announced, "I am going away." As his words struck her heart, he added, "But someday I will come again for you. And when I do, I will make you my bride. I promise." She believed him.

No one else in the mountain country did, however. Her family, especially her brothers, and the rest of the community were certain that this stranger had deceived a naive young girl. As time passed and the shepherd still had not returned, her brothers taunted her. "Why are you wasting your life waiting for that worthless shepherd? He doesn't love you. He probably has another girl, if he's not already married and raising a family! Get on with your life! Face reality!"

Though he was gone for a very long time, she trusted him. She knew him. His words rang strong and sure. She not only remembered the things he had told her, but the manner in which he had said them. Calm, confident … passionate. He had looked her in the eyes and said, "Please believe me. I won't lie to you. I am going to prepare a place for you, for us, to share our love forever. Wait for me." Those were his last words. And so she waited, enduring the ridicule and scorn.

One glorious day a huge cloud of dust rose over the horizon. People from all over the surrounding countryside came running to see what was happening. A royal procession from the capital, Jerusalem, appeared through the cloud! The king's bodyguards and then the king himself had stopped outside the Shulamite's vineyard. To the wonder of the young shepherdess, the front riders of the king's court arrived at the gate with a decree. "The king has asked for you!"

"For me?" she asked.

"Yes, for you. Come immediately."

In obedience, she followed. The crowds, including her brothers, watched as she drew near the royal carriage. As is the custom of the Orient, she bowed her head and fell upon her knees before the king.

He reached down, and with a gentle hand lifted her face until her eyes met his. Behold! She gazed into the face of her shepherd, the one who had won her heart. And she declared to all who listened, *"I am my beloved's, and my beloved is mine!"*[1]

FIRST, LOVE

"**I** am my beloved's ... my beloved is mine." Was that just a fairy tale? Did people ever really talk like that, think like that? Was there ever time to walk through the countryside? To allow love to ripen slowly like new fruit warmed by the sun? To wait patiently for a beloved's return or a dream to be realized?

Is it possible to know such love, commitment, and patience? To have such a passion for life that even in the face of opposition, a burdensome workload, and pressing needs, there is still hope and a sure knowledge that a grander purpose is being fulfilled? Is it possible to live with the anticipation that something wonderful is about to happen? Is there a "beloved" relationship in your life, leading you on a romantic adventure? Or are your hopes and dreams smothered in busyness?

We're all so busy just trying to get through our "to do" lists every day that we've forgotten how to live.

I happened to overhear a young couple one day, sitting out on the sidewalk of a popular coffee bar. Their organizer notebooks, cell phones, and beepers were sprawled on the café table between them.

"OK, I have Tuesday free," she said.

"Nope," he responded, "that won't work for me. How about Wednesday at 3:30?"

"No, I have to be at that meeting."

He leaned back, sighed, ran his fingers though his hair, and said, "We're just too busy ... by the way, who's picking up the kids tonight?"

I could relate. I've been there before, so much on the run that I barely have time to articulate the questions lingering in the back of my mind: "What am I doing here? Is this what life is all about?"

I'm afraid "busy" has replaced "beloved" as a description of who we are, how we see ourselves, and how we conduct ourselves—and this busyness has left us with a score of question marks dangling over our lives.

How do we rediscover "beloved"? Can we rekindle our childhood dreams? How do we live with passion? Is there a way to balance work, play, peace, excitement, joy, and sorrow?

HOLY QUEST

One night as a young boy, I discovered love. Lying on the grass in my backyard, I gazed upward, awestruck by the beauty of the heavens. My head and heart were spilling over with ideas. I felt like Lancelot and the Knights of the Round Table, in search of the Holy Grail. I too had a calling, a mission, a holy passion for life—and I could hardly wait to begin.

Earlier that day, I had walked down the aisle of an old theater in El Cajon, California, and made a commitment to God. Little did I know when my mom told me and my brothers we could go to the movies that day, that my life would be changed forever. I just wanted to see James Bond. Instead, there was Billy Graham preaching on the silver screen. After I got over my disappointment, I began to listen. I figured it was better than being home doing chores.

What the man said made sense. The whole universe seemed to change as I recognized that God is real and that He loves me.

With that walk forward, I began a journey of love, of faith, of life itself. Oh, I know that sounds grandiose and idealistic—it was. I was eleven years old and had met the living God. I felt like Charlton Heston playing Moses on the mountain, his face glowing. I had discovered what the Bible meant by "first love" and learned what others meant by "falling in love with God."

Thirty years later, I still believe that a relationship with God is like a grand, lifelong romance—and that He does the pursuing. God romances us. He woos us and demonstrates in multitudes of ways how much He loves us. No love relationship, however, is without its infatuating highs and heart-wrenching lows, but the sweetness of that love, the fulfillment, the hope, the passion for living—I am convinced it is the only way to be truly alive.

During my studies in the following years, I met one character who not only inspired my romantic notions, but also served as a great balancer, with his earthy, practical wisdom. Solomon knew romance with its high, lofty ideals, yet also understood the wisdom that flows out of living a life inspired by God's love.

Solomon lived with passion. He experienced the heights of divine intimacy, in a deep relationship with God—only to squander that relationship in carnal pleasure. He gained unparalleled wealth, then watched it all unravel, and pronounced all that he possessed as mere "vanity of vanities." He loved with purity—and succumbed to lust. He found intimate companionship in true love, yet suffered heartache and loneliness. He was the wisest of men—and yet he played the fool.

Each chapter of this book opens with a scenario out of Solomon's life, based on Scripture, and embellished with a little imagination on my part, in an attempt to understand the reality of Solomon's life, because I find hope in Solomon's experiences. In the end, Solomon found his way home—and left behind directions for us to follow through his writings and his example. He is a classic illustration of someone whose life was shaped and directed by God's passion for him.

Do you long to renew a weary faith? Do you hunger for a passion for living? Do you desire to see dormant gifts and talents revived? I've listed a lot of questions in this introduction—questions that I believe all of us raise in moments of doubt and despair. This book is for all who long for their hearts to be ignited by the holy flame of God's divine passion. "For the love of God has been poured out in our hearts," His Word tells us (see Romans 5:5). He wants us to *experience* that love!

In Solomon's book of *Proverbs*, Wisdom cries out to us, pleading with us to listen, to learn, to discover the depths of her treasures. Finally, she declares, *"I love those who love me, and those who seek me diligently will find me. ... whoever finds me finds life"* (8:17,35).

It's time to go find life.

Part One
PASSION

The power of the soul for good is in proportion to the strength of its passion.

—Coventry Patmore, 1895

Chapter One
BELOVED

SOLOMON watched the servants hover around the king's bed, covering him with warm blankets, fussing, trying to make his father comfortable. He shivered in sympathy as David struggled with the cold. One of the servants finally requested permission to find a young virgin to lie by the king and warm him.

Solomon knew of only one virgin beautiful enough, suitable enough. Abishag. The Shulamite.

King David was dying. Solomon wanted him comforted, but was relieved to realize that Abishag would only be a companion, not a lover.

Outside the quiet vigil, Solomon knew a political storm threatened. While Adonijah, David's older son, plotted to seize the throne, Nathan, the prophet, and Solomon's mother, Bathsheba, moved quickly to thwart the uprising. Both assured Solomon that David's desire—indeed, God's desire—was for Solomon to rule.

Even in his dying frailty, David was a powerful man. Solomon wondered if he could ever earn the same respect. All his life, Solomon witnessed his father's passion for his God, admired *his leadership of his people, and trusted him for his honor and integrity.*

But he also knew the history of his own birth, and it amazed him. His mother must have been extraordinary. David could have had any woman he wanted, besides the wives and concubines he already possessed. Solomon knew the privileges of royalty. But David wanted Bathsheba, and had committed murder and adultery to have her.

Both parents, each in their time and manner, shared their grief with him over the death of his brother, their first child. David accepted this loss as a consequence of his sin, using the story to remind Solomon again and again, "Keep the ways of the Lord your God ... keep His statutes, keep His commandments."

They told him how their sorrow was eased by his birth. They named him Solomon, and in the naming, placed their hopes for peace, health, and prosperity. Much of his education and training was based on the promise Bathsheba had extracted from David: that, in spite of the king's other sons, Solomon would one day be king. David knew the depth of God's grace and forgiveness—that if Solomon was God's choice, no measure of human sin could hinder His will.

Now the time was about to come. His father's words lingered in his mind, burned in his heart. He was not just inheriting a throne, he was taking the mantle of God upon his shoulders.

Solomon recognized now what David had been teaching him all along: his authority and power as a ruler would be a holy anointing, not just a political one. David's strength was spiritual. "My son, Solomon," David had said to him once, "know the God of your father." Know God. Solomon marveled again at the intimacy of David's relationship with the Lord. His father, unlike anyone else he knew, loved God with a fervor that set him apart from other men and enabled him to accomplish what others could only dream of.

"Know the God of your father, and serve Him with a loyal heart and with a willing mind; for the Lord searches the heart and understands all the intent of the thoughts. If you seek Him, He will be found by you; but if you forsake Him, He will cast you off forever. Consider now, for the Lord has chosen you."

With those words, David handed Solomon the plans for the temple he had hoped to build, and with them, the kingdom.

Solomon knew his youth had ended. He would soon be king.

Knowing the political battles and feeling the weight of his future responsibilities, he allowed himself a few moments to escape into thoughts of the Shulamite girl. The love he had discovered as a young man in the vineyards of Ephraim could now be fulfilled. He intended to return as king and reclaim his love. He pushed aside a moment of envy when he thought of her being brought to court to comfort David ... he could wait.

Now, he prayed to be ready. If he had learned anything at all from his father, it was that without a passion for God and for life, nothing would succeed.[1]

§

---

[1] *This scenario is based on 1 Kings, chapters one and two. As for the Shulamite, I am dramatizing Solomon's relationship with her—and will continue to do so in future chapters—based on research that raises the possibility that Abishag the Shunammite (which is synonymous with Shulamite) was Solomon's beloved.*

THE BEGINNING OF PASSION

Sometimes I think David felt sorry for God.

He had conquered Jerusalem, made the city his capital, and now lived in a beautiful palace on Mount Zion, built for him by Hiram, the king of Tyre. He enjoyed the fruits of living as a conquering hero—until he realized one day that the ark of the Lord rested behind mere tent curtains.

He ran to his chief prophet, Nathan, and shared his vision to build a new and glorious home for God. Nathan immediately smiled and said, "Of course, David! The Lord is with you! Do what you want!"

But that night God intervened, giving Nathan a difficult message to deliver to his king: "You have shed too much blood and have fought many wars; you shall not build a house for My name" (see 1 Chronicles 28:3).

From his political enemies to Bathsheba's husband, Uriah, David had fought and killed to hold onto his power. God's denial surely caused him grief and guilt as he recalled the years of war, the lives he had taken, and the treachery that had destroyed good men.

But that's not the end of the story. Though God did not allow David to build Him a house, the Lord intended to build David a house.

"The Lord Himself will establish a house for you," continued Nathan. "When you rest with your fathers, I will raise up your offspring … I will establish your kingdom. He is the one who will build a house for My name, and I will establish the throne of his kingdom forever. I will be his Father and he will be My son" (see 2 Samuel 7:12–14).

Do you know that the very first words of the New Testament are *"a record of the genealogy of Jesus Christ, **the son of David** ... "* (Matthew 1:1 NIV, emphasis added)? The angel who appeared to Mary also proclaimed, *"You will conceive in your womb and bring forth a Son, and shall call His name JESUS. He will be great, and will be called the Son of the Highest; and the Lord God will give Him the throne of **His father David"*** (Luke 1:31-32, emphasis added).

It was out of David's house, the one that God fashioned, that the promised Messiah would come into the world. The shepherd king who loved God with all his heart wanted to do something significant for the Lord. But God had a plan to do something wonderful for and through David.

David is not so different from the rest of us, is he? We want to do something great—for God or for mankind—but in spite of our good intentions, somehow our efforts fall apart. What we don't always realize is that the Lord wants to do something great for us. God proved through David that it is His intention to do for us what we cannot do for ourselves.

David hoped to build a house of stone, a place for God's love to dwell. But God intended to build a house of flesh and blood in the person of Jesus Christ, born to the house of David centuries after David left this world. Through Jesus, the most passionate and intimate love the world would ever know was manifested. The power of His love changed the human race forever as God's passion for us reached its ultimate expression.

David's intentions were good. But oh how much greater are God's intentions toward us! David preceded and set the stage for Solomon to learn the same lessons on an even grander scale.

LEARNING PASSION

> Even he who is lost through passion has not lost so much as he who has lost passion, for the former had possibility.
>
> —Søren Kierkegaard

Most of us yearn to "think big," to live passionate, large, exuberant lives. But, there's a part of us that's afraid. We want our passions in small, safe doses. We even wonder if a passionate, larger life just might be too sinful and indulgent. I agree with Jonathan Mayhew (a seventeenth century preacher), who observed, "No passion or affection, with which we are born, can be in itself sinful; it becomes so only by willful or careless indulgence."[2]

I believe that God *intended* us to live passionately, strong in our convictions, willing to be stretched in faith and in love. The English writer Dorothy Sayers argued, "The only sin passion can commit is to be joyless."

Solomon lived passionately. He learned from his father; David's passions elevated him and defeated him. Both Solomon and David allowed their passions to get them in trouble by "willful or careless indulgence." But when rooted in *spiritual* passion, their strong desires gave both men an enormous capacity to enjoy human love, and to create beautiful expressions of their faith, like David's Psalms and the beauty of Solomon's temple. Both served their people with grand vision.

Passion is a *learned* response. Just as we learn to think and communicate from our earthly parents, we also learn about spiritual love from our heavenly Father. Each of us is born with unique passions. Sometimes we're afraid of them, believing they can lead us to ruin. But couldn't they also be gifts from God, designed to make our lives richer?

We are consistently reminded throughout Scripture how much God wants to enrich and enlighten us. *"I bow my knees to the Father,"* Paul wrote to the Ephesians, *"that Christ may dwell in your hearts through faith; that you, being rooted and grounded in love, may be able to comprehend ... the width and length and depth and height—to know the love of Christ ..."* (3:14,17–19). Larger, deeper, stronger, higher. God pours His love into us. He causes our relationship with Him to grow, and with it, our view of life.

Because Solomon's name is almost synonymous with wisdom, we can hardly discuss him without contemplating his wisdom. But first, we need to step back a pace and discover what Solomon learned: that before wisdom can influence our lives, something deeper needs to take place. *Wisdom has to be ignited by passion.* "A man without passion is only a latent force, only a possibility, like a stone waiting for the blow from the iron to give forth sparks," wrote Swiss philosopher Henri Frederic Amiel.

But who strikes the blow? Who ignites the passion?

I learned, after trying too many times to muster up passion on my own, that the source of true passion is God Himself, the "lover of my soul." His passion for us, like life breathed into us, begets all that is good. His wisdom flows out of His love, and in turn guides us and teaches us how to live as a "beloved one."

Solomon's wisdom, without his passion, is just a set of nice platitudes for living. Bumper sticker material.

What's behind all those wise sayings? Our first clues are found in one of the most poetic expressions of human and spiritual love ever penned, the *Song of Solomon.*

A Book of Passion

The average person goes to his grave with his music still in him.

—Oliver Wendell Holmes

Solomon's music flowed out of him, prolifically. He wrote some three thousand proverbs and over one thousand songs (1 Kings 4:32). In Scripture, his wisdom and poetry are compiled into the books of *Proverbs, Ecclesiastes,* and the *Song of Solomon.*

Called the most misunderstood book in Scripture, the *Song of Solomon* is also one of the most beloved. The love story between Solomon and the Shulamite girl has intrigued readers for centuries.

Jewish rabbis once debated whether Solomon's *Song* could be legitimately included in the canon of Scripture because the language is so earthy, sensuous, and graphic. The early Jews would not allow their young men to read the book until they were thirty years old.

In the original Hebrew, the language can make you blush. Even in today's permissive world, we are unaccustomed to explicit sexual language in a religious context. But the Hebrew culture didn't separate spirituality and sensuality the way we do—Solomon certainly didn't. God gave us five senses to see, hear, taste, touch, and smell, and when these senses are used in harmony with God's revelation, this too can be part of our spiritual experience.

Some friends recently attended a funeral service at a traditional Greek Orthodox Church. A young wife and mother had been tragically killed in an auto accident; the family's grief was nearly unbearable. My friends were struck by the style of mourning. Wailing and crying out loud, moaning, and passionate, verbal expressions of sorrow punctuated the otherwise formal ceremony. Neither the family members nor the priests were at all disturbed or surprised by the continuous wailing. Indeed, it became the background music for a ceremony of sorrow.

Having conducted many funeral services, I've seen heavy, deep expressions of grief, but in our more reserved culture, we stifle our cries and attempt to shield those around us from the intensity of our emotions. In this Greek family, as in other cultures, passions, genuine and heartfelt, are allowed more freedom of expression, and no one—particularly the religious community—is shocked by them.

Similarly, Solomon held nothing back in describing the fervency of his love and attraction to his beautiful Shulamite girl.

In his book, *Jesus Man of Joy*, Sherwood Wirt wrote: "Until one has absorbed the Song verse by verse, in all its exotic and erotic flavor and mysterious references, one cannot fully appreciate what it has to do with joy ... it radiates expressions of warm affection, using the imagery of flowers and fruits, gardens and perfumes, wind and water, fields and mountains, spices and jewelry ... the total effect is enchanting."[3]

As you read these passionate and tender expressions of love, read the words not just with your mind, but also with your heart. Allow yourself to be carried away by the poetry of language.

> I am my beloved's and my beloved is mine. ... (Song 6:3)

> Many waters cannot quench love, nor can the floods drown it. ... (8:7)

> Make haste, my beloved, and be like a gazelle or a young stag on the mountain of spices. (8:14)

Of the three books of the Bible attributed to Solomon, the *Song* is traditionally last in order. But in following Solomon's life and writing, I decided to begin with his love song, because in many ways, that's where his story begins.

LOVE OF ALL LOVES

When Solomon fell in love, he wrote the original fairy tale. It's all there: a beautiful, young, virginal woman with a difficult life; a handsome prince, identity unknown; the beautiful, poetic language of rapturous new love; the conflict of separation, with promises for the future; her family's distrust; his return to claim her as his bride. It's the formula for every fairy tale that came after; it's *Sleeping Beauty, Cinderella*, and the great romances all rolled into one.

The *Song of Solomon* is different from any other book in the Bible. There is a straightforward interpretation, the story of Solomon and the Shulamite girl. But there are also layers of meaning, some of which only became obvious as time unfolded new revelations. This very poetic yet practical book has been described as a fragile flower that requires careful handling.

Let's unfold that flower and look at the four most accepted interpretations of Solomon's love song:

SOLOMON IN LOVE

The book is first a love story. Early Jewish teachers regarded it as a simple volume, dedicated to the Lord and devoted to understanding human love. Wedded life in Israel represented the highest, deepest, and most respectful form of affection. The *Song of Solomon* expresses the heart of a satisfied husband and devoted wife.

During this time in history, particularly in the nations surrounding Israel, women were viewed as property—as goods and services. The Jewish culture, in view of God's revelation in their lives, elevated the role of women. Hebrew Scriptures taught, *"Then God said, 'Let Us make man in Our image, according to Our likeness;' ... So God created man in His own image; in the image of God He created him; male and female He created them"* (Genesis 1:26–27).

The *Song's* expression of wedded love includes a healthy view of sex, which Solomon was not shy about describing. Marriage counselors often encourage couples to read the *Song of Solomon* together, to open up communication, and to enable husbands and wives to freely express their love for each other. It's proven to be a popular counseling technique!

GOD IN LOVE WITH ISRAEL

The Jewish people sometimes called the *Song* the Book of Communion. Through the centuries, the more spiritually-minded teachers recognized a deeper meaning in the lyrical words: God describing His matchless love for the nation of Israel. The prophets portrayed Jehovah as the bridegroom and Israel as the bride; Solomon's words painted a beautiful picture of a nation living in happy communion with its God. The language of intimacy became an allegory of the kind of intimacy God desires to have with His people.

JESUS IN LOVE WITH HIS CHURCH

When Jesus Christ established His Church, the revelation of God was extended beyond the Jewish nation to all nations, all people. Jesus is the heavenly Bridegroom, and the Bride of Christ is the Church, made up of people from all backgrounds and walks of life.

The Bible teaches that one day Jesus will come back to take His Church home with Him—to the marriage supper of the Lamb! A wedding feast!

"Then I saw heaven opened," wrote the apostle John, *"and behold, a white horse! He who sat upon it was called Faithful and True, ..."*

(Revelation 19:11 RSV). Do you see a pattern here? The prince returning on a white horse? Now you know where all the old fairy tales got their original ideas.

GOD'S PASSIONATE LOVE FOR US

Now we come full circle. We come back to the intimate one-on-one love relationship, only this time it is between the individual believer and the Lord.

Some of us, especially men, have a hard time relating to "falling in love" in spiritual terms. "Falling in love with God" seems peculiar, even strange.

It is, to our human understanding. Which is why discovering such a relationship with the God who created us is nothing short of a divine revelation. It's not wimpy or weird to love God with a passionate heart, but it is foreign to our natural way of thinking.

God desires that our faith be based on His love for us. Instead, we have turned this beautiful relationship into a religious exercise that shackles us to rules and laws that we can never keep, despite our best efforts.

J. Vernon McGee described it this way: "People are being deluded. They feel that living the Christian life is like following the instructions for putting together a toy ... a little mixture of psychology, a smattering of common sense, a dash of salesmanship and a few verses of the Bible as a sugarcoating for the whole thing, makes a successful formula for Christian living. ... My friend, I say to you, what we need is a relationship with Jesus Christ. We need a hot passion for Him."[4]

The love between God and His children has motivated many a believer to fall on his knees and exclaim, "I am my Beloved's, and my Beloved is mine." We are beloved! It's time we realize it.

What Is Your Song?

William Olney, a dear friend of C.H. Spurgeon and the senior deacon of the Metropolitan Tabernacle, had died. During the funeral address, Mr. Spurgeon described his passing: "He died full of life."[5]

I've asked myself many times: If my days were up tomorrow, would I die "full of life"? Or would I be more like the person who "goes to his grave with his music still in him"?

That's why Solomon's *Song* has captured the hearts of believers in a unique manner, different from any other portion of Scripture. It answers the yearnings of our hearts and gives us a love song to sing—even in this fallen world. From Genesis to Revelation, we can hear the story, resounding through the ages, of the Shepherd who came down from the mountain heights of glory into the lives of those who yearn for love. There He fell in love with His beloved, His own creation, and sought to win her love, this bride who so often has thought herself unworthy. Falling in love with the Shepherd, we discover Him to be the King of kings and Lord of lords, who gave His life for us, desiring to fill us with love and joy, and prepared to carry us into eternity.

This is the ultimate romance!

Come Away, My Love

Before we move on in Solomon's life, I hope you'll stop to meditate on these four thoughts:

§   The Shulamite girl felt unlovely and unworthy. Yet, Solomon looked at her with eyes of love and saw only her beauty and potential. That's how Jesus sees us. *"While we were still sinners, Christ died for us,"* Romans 5:8 tells us. Proof of

His love lies in the scars of the Cross, the marks of His passion, which He bore on His body.

§   God desires to pour blessings into receptive hearts. He desires to lavish us with His holy gifts. *"Eye has not seen, nor ear heard, nor have entered into the heart of man the things which God has prepared for those who love Him,"* wrote the apostle Paul (1 Corinthians 2:9).

§   The Lord wants to bring you into a love relationship that will enrich your life in ways you cannot even begin to fathom! Ultimately, there is nothing greater than love, and what you experience vertically in a relationship with God will spill over into your relationships with other people. When you have known deep spiritual love, nothing else—be it wine, drugs, worldly appetites, riches, or success—can bring you the same sense of satisfaction.

§   We never need to be afraid to follow Him. The Good Shepherd will never lead us astray. Solomon left his love for a time, promising her he would return. No one else believed him, but she did. She trusted his love. How much more then can we trust in our heavenly Shepherd to return as He said He would, and to lead us into green pastures and clean, refreshing pools of water to nourish our souls?

Solomon found love *away* from the politics and burdens of his court. In the countryside where the vineyards grow, love blossomed, unhindered by worldly distractions. Similarly, Christ longs to call us away from the trivial things of this world into a deeper communion with Him. *"I have come that they may have life and that they may have it more abundantly,"* He said (John 10:10b).

Doesn't that amaze you? Life abundantly ... *plentiful, bountiful, more than enough, large, great, rich, lavish, productive, exuberant.*

Would you describe your existence in those terms? Can you apply those words to your daily living?

Are you ready to accept God's invitation to live such a life? *Come*, He says, *let's find out what life and love are all about.*

Rise up, my love ... and come away. For lo, the winter is past, the rain is over and gone. The flowers appear on the earth; the time of singing has come, and the voice of the turtledove is heard in the land. The fig tree puts forth her green figs, and the vines with tender grapes give a good smell. Rise up my love, my fair one, and come away!

—Song 2:10–13

Chapter Two
CONSUMING PASSION

*T*HE *procession to Gibeon snaked through the desert slowly this time. The extra livestock added to the dust of the long caravan of servants, animals, and courtiers. Solomon rode ahead on his horse, hoping for solitude.*

His thoughts turned often toward the Shulamite. He allowed himself a few moments to savor her memory, smiling as he remembered the poetic words he heard himself uttering as they sat in the garden. "Behold, you are fair, my love! Behold, you are fair! You have dove's eyes."

He forced himself to redirect his thoughts. This was no time to indulge his romantic daydreams. Since those last private moments with his father, there had been no time to think.

David's final words to him had ignited months of bloodshed, political posturing, and ruthless decisions—even a political marriage with the Pharaoh's daughter. When David was put to rest, Solomon was like a racehorse let out of the gates.

"Be strong and prove yourself a man. ..." Have I done that,

father? he wondered. "Keep the charge of the Lord your God: to walk in His ways, to keep His statutes, ..." Have I kept your counsel?

Today he intended to honor the Lord. A thousand animals waited dumbly to be slaughtered on the high altar. Solomon welcomed the time to think and pray. Maybe better not to think ... ascending David's throne, wrestling sovereignty from his calculating brothers, taming the politically minded priests and those who challenged his right to be king ... just recalling recent events exhausted him.

The constant presence in the court of his mother, Bathsheba—his most loyal ally—reminded him of his anointing. Solomon needed this time, this pilgrimage. Perhaps in Gibeon he would meet the Almighty.

As soon as the caravan arrived, the work began. The shrieks of slaughtered livestock rose above the hurried orders; quickly, the blood was thrown onto the bronze altar, while the animals were gutted. His congregation watched as Solomon gave animal after animal to the consuming fire, their praise and adoration rising with each surge of flames. A thousand sacrifices spewed the stench and smoke over the city like the holocaust of sin upon a nation.

Each offering reminded Solomon of the families ... the tribes ... the millions of people who would look to him. He pictured them, the children of Israel, needing a king, a sacrificial leader and servant of the Almighty. He could offer sacrifices ... but could he offer himself?

By nightfall, he was spent. Closing his eyes in weary sleep, he felt even more exhausted as he realized his unworthiness for the task ahead.

He still thought of himself as a child, not a king. He grieved for his father, and thought about how much the king had loved his Lord. It was a relationship Solomon had observed from a distance—even envied. Tonight, in spite of the hours of sacrifice, in spite of his efforts to keep the law, the distance still seemed so great ... how would he get there?

He began to weep and couldn't stop. Tears washed down his face, taking with them the lingering smell of fire. His absolute weariness disturbed his sleep.

"Have mercy on me, O God." He remembered the words David had sung in the night, on many occasions during Solomon's life. "I will take refuge in the shadow of Your wings ... my heart is steadfast, O Lord ... for great is Your love, reaching to the heavens; Your faithfulness reaches to the skies. Be exalted, O God ... let Your glory be over all the earth ... Hear my cry, O God," Solomon pleaded silently, "listen to my prayer."[6]

The haunting images of sacrifices consumed by fire, swallowed up by heat and smoke were suddenly, in Solomon's dreams, themselves burned away by an even holier fire. The Almighty's love, reaching to the heavens ... exalted over all the earth ... all-consuming, poured into Solomon's heart ... answering his father's prayers.

In that mysterious moment of consciousness halfway between sleep and wakefulness, Solomon experienced a revelation. No longer was the Lord distant. No longer was Solomon mystified by David's passion. God's love poured over him like the cleansing tears that poured down his face. He cried with joy. The holocaust was gone.

"All my heart and soul," he prayed, "are Yours."[7]

§

The Lord startled Solomon out of his sleep that night by coming to him in a dream and answering his cry with a question: *"Ask! What shall I give you?"* (1 Kings 3:5).

Even a day earlier, Solomon might have answered differently. But the day of sacrifice had left Solomon overwhelmed. Drowning in a sea of responsibilities, he was too weary to ask for anything but help. God anticipated Solomon's humble state and made Himself available for whatever Solomon needed. The Lord, who once revealed Himself to Moses as the great "I AM" now revealed Himself to Solomon as *Jehovah Jireh*, the LORD-Will-Provide (Genesis 22:14).

A.W. Tozer once said, "It is doubtful whether God can bless a man greatly until He has hurt him deeply."[8] Solomon's life, I imagine, had been a satisfying and content one until David's death. He was a beloved son and a prince with unlimited resources and few restrictions.

Now the well-being of God's people depended upon his leadership. He was scared, unsure of himself, and realized he wasn't ready for the task.

A greedier man would have asked for power and wealth. A prouder man would have presumed he could handle it. A less intelligent man would have believed he was smart enough to succeed on his own.

Broken and filled with the love God had poured upon him, Solomon instead responded, *"Now, O LORD my God, you have made your servant king in place of my father David. But I am only a little child and do not know how to carry out my duties. So give your servant a discerning heart to govern your people and to distinguish between right and wrong. For who is able to govern this great people of yours?"* (1 Kings 3:7,9 NIV).

Solomon began to grasp, perhaps for the first time, the true nature of God. Rather than a God who demanded a performance from Solomon, who held him to overwhelming expectations, God offered Himself. He reached out to meet the needs of His child.

Solomon has often been applauded for making the right choice in asking for wisdom. But in reality, he was responding to God's offer. Solomon reached out and received what the Lord wanted to give him.

God gave him a wise and understanding heart—*"so that there has not been anyone like you before you, nor shall any like you arise after you"* (1 Kings 3:10)—and He blessed him with everything else as well: prosperity, success—and a *passion* to know Him.

DANGEROUSLY GIFTED

Solomon had been given a rare gift, out of which grew his enormous success. His passion for taking everything he tackled to the highest level of achievement was only equaled by his genius and insight. But somehow, at some point, everything went awry. What happened? How does such great talent get turned?

Take a more modern example. Jacqueline du Pre was called classical music's golden girl. When she made music with her cello, her blonde hair flew, her body moved to the music and "the passion in her playing stirred the hearts of her listeners."[9]

As a teenager, she dazzled concertgoers and began moving in the same circles as musicians like Arthur Rubenstein and Itzhak Perlman. But when multiple sclerosis struck du Pre at age 28, her music was prematurely silenced, and her fans were devastated. The disease took its toll physically and psychologically, twisting the rest of her life into a melodrama of family frictions, scandal, and declining health.

One journalist described Jacqueline du Pre as "dangerously gifted."

How does someone end up "dangerously gifted"? Why does this sound so familiar? As much as we admire genius—even envy it—Jacqueline du Pre's story is sadly typical. A grand passion for a particular gift or skill can become so consuming that an individual's life careens out of balance. Everything else—family, friends, and other relationships—is sacrificed on the altar of individual genius. We explain away the excesses of rock stars, and the tortured souls of eccentric artists and depressed writers by romanticizing their troubles, chalking them up to "creative genius."

Even when we look apprehensively at those whose legendary passions turned into destructive forces, don't we still secretly yearn for something similar to spring up into our daily routines? Don't we desire a grand passion, a calling, a reason to live that is both consuming and compelling? Don't we long for life with a purpose, something to stave off the boredom and senseless busyness? Aren't we all looking for something, somewhere, somehow to bring romance and adventure into our lives?

But what happens if we find such a grand passion? How do we live with it without being burned—and burning others? When Winston Churchill led his nation's fight for freedom against the evil of Nazism, he spoke of possessing an extraordinary sense of destiny. Yet, he later acknowledged, "I know what it is to be consumed."[10]

And what happens if the gift, the calling, or the reason fails us? What if, as in Jacqueline du Pre's case, illness steals away our ability and leaves us empty and tormented with loss? What if the music fails, the play flops, or the war ends in tragedy? Even our most triumphant moments here on earth can end on a bittersweet note.

Os Guinness proposes this solution: "For some people the grand passion is art, music, or literature; for others the dream of freedom or justice; for yet others the love of a man or a woman. But search as you will, there is no higher or more ultimate passion than a human being ablaze with a desire for God."[11]

And what sets the human heart ablaze? Nothing inflames a man's heart and soul more than understanding God's passion for him.

CONSUMING LOVE

The *Song of Solomon* is a love story, both earthly and spiritual, told in the passionate language of a consuming relationship. Solomon's ode to love epitomizes ultimate passion on many different levels.

> He brought me to the banqueting house, and his banner over me was love. Sustain me with cakes of raisins, refresh me with apples, for I am lovesick.
>
> —Song 2:4–5

Lovesick! Being so enthralled, and so consumed with love that you don't want to eat or sleep—you even feel sick—doesn't seem spiritual at all. You become so enchanted with the beauty and character of this person, that everything in you is drawn to them. You dream of your love and nothing else; you are inspired and motivated by this relationship.

Cakes of raisins, in the verse above, is also interpreted "flagons of wine." In other words, a table of wine and feasting was laid before a loved one, enriching the senses and sustaining the body in the face of this powerful emotion.

This is exactly what God desires for us—to experience His love in such an intimate manner that we are completely satisfied, and have no fears about this grand passion fading away or turning into a destructive force in our lives. He wants us to be "ablaze with a desire for [Him]," as He nourishes our souls with the "wine" of His Spirit and the "bread" of His Word.

I have had many wonderful experiences in my walk with the Lord, but there are times when the Lord reveals Himself in a special way. On one occasion, while I prayed, I thought of how wonderful the Lord is. My thoughts were flooded with memories of God's love to me personally. So many answered prayers. So many miracles. So many promises. And when I thought of how *patient* God has been with me, I was simply overcome. The glory of the Lord filled my bedroom with such powerful *joy* that I laughed and cried. I will never forget that day, and the many outpourings of His love upon me since.

I try to imagine sometimes what the apostle Paul experienced when he was caught up to the third heaven (see 2 Corinthians 12). "Inexpressible" is one description he used. This wonderful love of God is a paradox. We long for it, and yet the glory of it all is more than we can bear.

Have you ever felt so in love with a person, a calling, or life itself that the joy almost seemed unbearable? This is the kind of passion God has for us through the Holy Spirit. Wonderful, overwhelming, and ultimately life-sustaining. Our relationship with God is a grand love affair. Every beautiful love relationship you've ever personally enjoyed is a reenactment of an old story—we love Him because He first loved us.

A Jewish Wedding

There she is. Finally! The most beautiful vision I have ever seen. Her hair is deep chestnut with a gentle roll, pulled back on one side, a gardenia tucked behind one ear. As she walks down the aisle toward me in a cream-colored, form-fitting dress, some seven hundred witnesses, our friends and family, rejoice with me, basking in the radiance of her princess smile.

She looks at me, and I understand Solomon's burst of poetic emotion: "O my love, you are beautiful!" (see Song 6:4). It is August 5, 1977—my wedding day.

Twenty-two years later, my wife and daughter are in the dining room laughing as they make plans for my daughter's upcoming wedding. I can't believe it; I am now *the father of the bride!*

I am amazed at the sudden flurry of activity around our house—the shopping trips, the phone calls, the occasional budget checks with Dad (my main function at this point). So many arrangements—so little time.

Weddings are landmark occasions, steeped in tradition and symbolism, which is why I love the classic story of the Jewish wedding.

In ancient Jewish culture, marriages were arranged. Families who knew and respected each other made the arrangements, often while their sons and daughters were young. These marriages actually did very well—apparently better than our modern ones.

We cherish the notion of falling in love, and being led by our emotions. But some cultures believe that love will be *learned*, with a strong commitment and enough time.

I can picture a rather nervous young man, sent by his father to visit his fiancée's house (sometimes their first meeting) to present his *covenant,* or the terms of his marriage proposal.

First, he negotiates the *dowry*. What is he willing to pay for his bride? Buying a bride may be strange to us, but it was actually quite practical. As an agricultural society, ancient Israel's economy depended on the entire family working. To recoup his losses when the girl leaves home, the father set a dowry price.

The asking price reflected the father's love; his way of saying, *When a man is willing to pay this price, his love is worthy of my daughter.*

Next, the bridegroom presents his vows of love, in front of the father, to the bride. From that day, the young couple is legally married, even though the consummation and wedding are still months away.

The bride and groom now drink a cup of wine together, sealing the covenant. The wine symbolizes his willingness to *sacrifice* for his bride and her acceptance of his proposal. Then the groom ceremoniously pays the dowry, literally paying a great price for the love of this young woman.

With all transactions completed, the groom speaks privately to his bride, as he prepares to leave:

> I must leave you now, my love. I am going to my father's house, to build us a bridal chamber, where we will share our honeymoon together. There, we will live and raise our children. When it is finished, I will return, and take you away with me to our wedding and new home. You have my promise.

Naturally, the bride eagerly asks, "When are you coming back? When is our wedding date?"

He replies, "I don't know the exact day, or even the hour. Only my father can determine that."

So, furiously, he returns to work on their future home, spurred on by the joy he anticipates for his wedding night. He knows that the bridal chamber will only be finished when his father says it's finished—for good reason. You can imagine that if it were left up to a young groom, he would throw up some little shack in a couple of days and say, "Let's get on with it!" Leaving it to the father's discretion meant that a real home, a truly magnificent mansion, would be built. Usually the groom built a separate house on his father's property over the course of twelve to eighteen months.

In the meantime, the bride waits for the day when her groom will come to capture her. She is confident of his return for two reasons: because of the vows he pledged and because of the price he paid. Meanwhile, she wears a veil of consecration, signifying to all potential suitors that she is taken.

She receives regular progress reports about her new home. A friendly messenger tells her the foundation had been laid. "The walls are up!" someone else announces. The doors are set. The flooring's down. Now the roof! In the closing days, her excitement grows. All the signs indicate that *any day* her beloved is coming, with his best man, to capture her. Then the wedding ceremony can begin!

The anticipation of the two families grows. Their households buzz with a flurry of activity.

The bride gathers her sisters and bridesmaids for nightly slumber parties. Their oil lamps are burning, as the girls take turns watching and waiting through the night. All that's left, according to custom, is for the father of the groom to give permission to his son *in the middle of the night* to go get his bride. At any moment, the groom could sweep them all up, and the joyous wedding ceremony will begin. The wait adds to the suspense, as well as the romance.

Picture now, the father, one evening, leaving his house and walking out into the cool night. It is a short distance to the new bridal chamber his son has worked so hard to finish. He stops to peer into his son's room and watches him sleep for a while. The young man barely stirs, so exhausted is he from twelve months of hard labor. The father smiles, his heart bursting with pride. This is the little boy who followed him everywhere, learned what he taught him, and bears his own image. The father is proud of how hard his son has worked. More than just the sweat of labor, he poured his very soul into this future home for his beloved. Nothing makes a father happier than to see his own son filled with joy. What a great gift he is now able to give his son.

He reaches down and shakes the young man's shoulder.

Moments later the groom dashes through the streets, yelling at the top of his lungs for his best man and the other young men of the bridal party. It's midnight! It's time! They run from house to house, growing in number as well as noise, shouting and racing as they head toward the other side of the village to the house of the bride.

It has to be done quickly. They don't want to lose the element of surprise. That's the romance of it all!

Typically, Jewish brides were "stolen." This tradition, passed on from mother to daughter, was kept alive by romantic tales told around the table at night. Little girls grew up with the fantasy of one day being *snatched away* and carried off into the night, not by a stranger, but by one who loved her so much that he paid a dear price to win her heart and her love.

As the groom and his friends come rushing in, the father of the bride and her brothers pretend not to see the intruders. They know the wedding party is ready to begin. The commotion, happy voices, and laughter waken the people in the village. They look out the window and see all the young people running with oil lamps. They may not know *who*, but they know *what*—a wedding is taking place! That's where today's tradition originated of honking horns and proclaiming to the world that a wedding is taking place.

While all this excitement is building, across the valley, two girls look with wide eyes out into the darkness. "It's time! It's time! They're coming!" they shriek with delight. They quickly awaken the bride to get her ready, because they know the groom will arrive shortly—"in the twinkle of an eye."

Laughter, shouting, hugging, kissing—the groom arrives, ready to take his bride home. Her father watches with the smile of a father watching his little girl being taken away by the man who loves her. He's pleased, a little sad, but content.

The wedding party finally reaches the groom's father's house, and the family gathers to begin a seven-day celebration. Realize, this is not an easy event to prepare for. A wedding was considered the single most important social event in the village and was a huge undertaking, providing for guests who are going to stay and have a good time for seven days. The host always worries about running out of food or wine. You can understand now how significant and beautifully symbolic it was for Jesus' first recorded miracle to be turning water into wine at a wedding in Cana.

The bride and groom are now ready to enter the bridal chamber and consummate their marriage, while the celebration outside continues for an entire week.

On the seventh day, the bride comes out with her groom to make a long awaited appearance, heralded by the joyful cheers of the crowd. Now comes the grand finale—*the marriage supper,* in honor of the new couple, a feast suitable for a king and queen, shared by family and friends on the eve of a new era.

Does all this ring any bells? When we come to the New Testament, or the New Covenant, we read that Jesus spoke these words the night before His crucifixion:

> Don't let your hearts be troubled. Trust in God, and trust in me. There are many rooms in my Father's house; I would not tell you this if it were not true. I am going there to prepare a place for you. After I go and prepare a place for you, I will come back and take you to be with me so that you may be where I am.
>
> —John 14:1–3 NCV

In John chapters 13–14, Jesus actually fulfills the three conditions of a Jewish wedding. He shares His vows through His promises. He even gives us the same promise earlier given to Solomon. *"And whatever you ask in My name, that I will do, that the Father may be glorified in the Son. If you ask anything in My name, I will do it"* (John 14:13–14).

He promised us the Holy Spirit: *"I will pray the Father, and He will give you another Helper, that He may abide with you forever … I will not leave you orphans"* (John 14:16,18). Finally, He promised us peace, *"Peace I leave with you, My peace I give to you; not as the world gives do I give to you. Let not your heart be troubled, neither let it be afraid"* (John 14:27).

Then, while celebrating the Passover, He drank a cup of wine, sealing His covenant with us. Later that evening, He went into the still, dark night to pay the greatest price ever paid for a bride. *He literally paid the price of His own life for the beloved of His soul.*

No wonder the crucifixion is described as the "passion of Christ," for truly it was.

THE GREATEST ROMANCE

One of the most dramatic moments in a traditional wedding is when the groom lifts the bride's veil and is told, "You may kiss the bride!"

Applause, laughter, and a few whoops and hollers erupt as the crowd rejoices in the public display of affection and commitment. Everyone knows what the ceremony symbolizes—the right for this man and woman to enter into the joy of marital intimacy.

Two thousand years ago, in another public display of love, Jesus died on a cross to pay the price for our sins. At the moment of His death, *"the veil of the temple was torn in two from top to bottom"* (Mark 15:38).

The Jewish people understood the two-fold significance of this supernatural act. The renting (tearing) of garments is a traditional symbol of mourning. God was mourning the death of His Son.

The veil of the temple covered the innermost part of the sanctuary, the part of the temple *"which is called the Holiest of All"* (Hebrews 9: 3). Only the high priest could enter into this holiest section of the tabernacle—the Holy of Holies. And even then, he could only enter once a year, bringing a blood offering for himself and his people.

When Jesus died, the supernatural renting in two of the thick, forbidding veil opened the entrance to the Holy of Holies, inviting the whole world to enter in. Jesus went before us as our High Priest, our sacrifice, and by offering Himself, He opened the door to a loving relationship that will satisfy, strengthen, and inspire us, not just for this life, but into eternity.

Jesus is the Bridegroom, who will appear one day at His Father's bidding, to snatch us away and bring us home to the most wonderful wedding supper ever planned. It's all there in the Gospels. The love, the romance, the wedding supper, and the consummation of becoming one with God in Holy Communion. It is the greatest passion, the most dramatic story, the deepest and the most enduring love we will ever know.

Chapter Three

LOVE THAT WON'T LET GO

*W*ʜᴇɴ *David died, it seemed as if the vortex of the universe shifted, and Solomon found himself in the whirlwind.*

He needed to find out where Abishag went. Thoughts of her slipped in and out of the shadows in his mind. He pronounced judgments and made rulings, exercising his gift from the Lord, watching his wisdom and wealth grow, relishing in the wonder of it. Even so, the Shulamite danced through his thoughts—and alongside her, memories of his brother, Adonijah.

"The kingdom was mine!"

Solomon could still hear Adonijah's bitter, complaining voice. His brother strutted through Israel, bragging about his right to be king, plotting, boasting, seizing what he believed should be his. Even Bathsheba finally took pity on him, but not until she had secured her own son's place on the throne.

Solomon remembered the day the city broke out in riotous celebration. As he rode David's mule up to the fountain at Gihon, laughter and blessings splashed out of the earth. People played their flutes, danced in the streets, and rejoiced until the noise rocked the ground. Zadok the priest held the tabernacle horn high over Solomon's head, while the rich, anointing oil glistened in the sun, flowing over his beard and hair. Zadok, Nathan the prophet, and all the people proclaimed, "Long live King Solomon!" and Solomon thought how completely glorious the day would have been—except for Adonijah.

Ruthless, conniving, handsome—Adonijah eerily resembled Absalom, David's oldest son, whose death had brought him such grief years ago. Solomon barely remembered him, but knew that Adonijah also emulated Absalom's lust for the throne.

"All of Israel expects me to be king," Adonijah had bragged to his band of ambitious followers. His hastily put together coup and victory feast excluded Solomon and the king's closest advisors. But the rest of his brothers and the king's servants had confidently raised their toasts as Adonijah declared himself king—until the uproar across town disrupted their party.

Solomon heard stories about the fear that struck Adonijah's guests. They realized, scrambling to safety, they were on the wrong side of David's power, at the wrong party, at the wrong time. He thought, wryly, of how quickly Adonijah bowed to David's wishes, running to the temple to find sanctuary and to declare his allegiance to his brother. "Indeed, Adonijah is afraid," his messengers told Solomon. He had no illusions, however, about his older brother's loyalty. He also knew that he would spare Adonijah's life as long as David lived.

But David died, and Solomon held the reins of power now. No one could be allowed to strain them too hard—especially Adonijah.

Bathsheba felt content, if wary, when Adonijah approached her. Prepared to be generous, eager to keep peace, she accepted his assurances that he came in peace. He just had one small request, nothing too significant; a consolation prize, really, she thought.

"Please speak to King Solomon," he appealed to her, "for he won't refuse you, that he might give Abishag the Shunammite as my wife."

Abishag, the girl who warmed David. The young woman's beauty and virgin innocence seemed to please everyone—David, Adonijah, even, Bathsheba noticed, Solomon, with his longing stares. Playing matchmaker would suit her.

Solomon realized how much his mother's request for an audience meant to her. He watched her take a deep breath, bow her head, then enter the court behind the Royal Guard. She had carefully dressed, and her attire enhanced the excitement he saw in her eyes as she looked up adoringly at him.

A warm smile creased his face as he stood respectfully to greet her, bowing as he gestured her toward the seat of honor at his right hand. She was enjoying the irony of being so formal with her own son, and he enjoyed the pleasure she took in being the king's mother.

"I desire a small petition of you; do not refuse me," she said directly.

"Ask it, my mother, for I will not refuse you."

So she said, "Let Abishag the Shunammite be given to Adonijah your brother as his wife."

Ah, so that was it. Adonijah's scheme.

Solomon's eyes narrowed, his muscles grew taut as he pictured Adonijah watching her and making his plans. When she came to court, her dark and enchanting beauty charmed every man. The form of her body was both young and mature, her mouth inviting ... Solomon had watched from a distance, knowing with satisfaction that other men might desire her, but he possessed her heart.

"Why would you request Abishag the Shunammite for Adonijah?" he responded, his voice growing louder as he heard her request echoed in his own words. "You might as well request the kingdom for him—after all, he is my older brother!" He swore with the Lord's name and cried, "May God deal with me, be it ever so severe, if Adonijah does not pay with his life for this request! And now, as surely as the Lord lives—He who established me securely on the throne of my father David and has founded a dynasty for me as He promised—Adonijah shall be put to death today!"

Solomon remembered now his own rage and fear. He could still see Bathsheba's surprised expression as he sent her away, berating her for underestimating Adonijah's treachery—then called for his captain to move swiftly.

Adonijah and Joab—David's loyal captain—both died that day. Solomon sought to protect his kingdom, convincing himself that Abishag's beauty had nothing to do with his rage. The kingdom was at risk ... he had to secure it ... it's what David would have wanted.

Was Adonijah's death necessary? He didn't really want to consider the matter, but sometimes at night, when he thought about the Shulamite, waiting for him in Ephraim, and dreamt of those quiet, innocent days in the vineyard, he wondered when there would be time to rekindle their love.[12]

§

JEALOUS LOVE

The love of God is a jealous love.

Jealousy? Is that a godly attribute? We can probably understand Solomon crashing around his kingdom, seeking vengeance, threatened by jealous rivalry—both for political power and for a beautiful woman. But God? Can you imagine Him as a jealous lover?

That's exactly what He is! *"For the LORD your God is a consuming fire, a jealous God"* (Deuteronomy 4:24), Moses taught the children of Israel. God's love is so rich, so high, and so deep that we cannot begin to fathom it—but it is a love that jealously desires our undivided hearts.

Jealousy comes in two forms: the sinful kind and the godly kind.

Adonijah seethed with jealousy over losing the kingdom to Solomon. He plotted a scheme that would advance his political position, and strike at Solomon's heart, by demanding Abishag. He even used Solomon's mother, Bathsheba, with no regard for her feelings. Self-interest completely fueled his bitter emotions.

Sinful jealousy displays a total lack of trust and understanding for the object of love. Selfish, self-seeking, self-preserving, it cares more for self than the other person.

Solomon was more complex. He loved the Shulamite girl, and he desired to rule his father's kingdom in a righteous manner. His anger and use of kingly power to put someone to death were fueled by jealous rage, but also by the need to secure his God-given position. Adonijah played with dangerous fire when he threatened both Solomon's kingdom *and* his love life.

But with God, the motives are pure. Moses explained, *"For you shall worship no other god, for the LORD, whose name is Jealous, is a jealous God"* (Exodus 34:14). God is jealous over us; He will not share us with another because He knows it is not in our best interest. He knows worldly passions can steal our hearts and hurt us.

"For love is strong as death," the Shulamite girl said to Solomon. *"Jealousy as cruel as the grave; its flames are flames of fire, a most vehement flame"* (Song 8:6). Again, this story of two lovers is a picture of God's love.

The Lord's emotional attitude toward you can only be described by fire. Hot, intense, and passionate! Yet so many people never experience this love. Henry David Thoreau wrote, "Most men lead lives of quiet desperation." I look around at our world and think, sadly, he's right.

Jesus wrote to the church in the book of Revelation, "I wish that you were hot or cold!" (see Revelation 3:15). Even people who are cold can at least be passionate about their bitterness and their unbelief. I believe Jesus implied that such people are actually closer to the kingdom of heaven because at least there is a spark of passion in their lives.

Think of the apostle Paul. He persecuted Christians with a hateful zeal that caused believers to fear the sound of his name. Yet, I can't help but think that this passion, misguided and misused as it was, made him more vulnerable to the blinding Light that struck him down on the road to Damascus.

"Because you are lukewarm," Jesus continued in Revelation, *"I will vomit you out of My mouth"* (3:16). I can't imagine a more graphic

picture of godly disdain. There is nothing worse than a human being made in the image of God who lives a passionless life. You were not made for such a bleak existence! In fact, it will drive you crazy! You were made to know God. Your body was created to house His glory. He jealously desires such a life for you!

If we knew a man who said, "It doesn't matter to me how my wife bestows her favors upon others. Why, I'm so large-hearted that I can share her with anyone," most of us would think that such a man doesn't really love his wife. He doesn't care who uses her, or how her emotions get tossed about.

Similarly, Paul the apostle, writing to the church in Corinth, said, *"I am jealous for you with godly jealousy"* (2 Corinthians 11:2). Because Paul cared so deeply for this flock of believers, he was saying, "I'm jealous for you, and because I'm jealous, if I see you getting off track, I'm going to confront you in love."

Dwight L. Moody, the great evangelist, preached on many subjects, but according to his biography, "he had one central message to share with the people: Men and women are all created to be friends and lovers of God. We are made for no other end. Until we realize this we will live lives of turmoil, confusion, and even desperation."[13]

We are made to be on a heavenly course, being drawn closer and closer to our heavenly Father.

LOVE STRONGER THAN DEATH

While they still courted in the vineyards of Ephraim, the Shulamite girl wrote to her beloved Solomon:

> Set me as a seal upon your heart, as a seal upon your arm; for love is as strong as death, its jealousy unyielding as the grave. It burns like blazing fire, like a mighty flame. Many waters cannot

quench love, nor can the floods drown it. If one were to give all
the wealth of his house for love, it would be utterly scorned.

—Song 8:6–7 NKJV and NIV

Just as death cannot be held back, she said, and as the grave waits
to hold us, so love can be equally powerful, equally inevitable. Two
potent forces—both capable of inciting joy and sorrow, anticipation
and fear—love and death are opposite ends of the spectrum that too
often come around to meet one another.

Different, yet alike—and the perceived "alikeness" is often what
makes us fear the intensity of true love, the love that is ultimately from
God. Fear and confusion are what can make us run from love, hold it
at arm's length, and fail to embrace it. But the alternative—the place
we find ourselves when we push love away—is best described by C.S.
Lewis: "The only place outside of Heaven where you can be perfectly
safe from all the dangers and perturbations of love is Hell."[14]

So there you have it. We either accept the seal of love, or we will be
burned by the fires of emptiness, loneliness, and self-hatred. The secret
is to learn the difference between love that is sure and godly and the
false love that is selfish and deceptive. One is possessive and destructive
and its end is sorrow, while the other brings life, joy, and completeness
into one's life. While we may fear death, our hearts long to embrace the
kind of strong, life-giving love that the Shulamite has offered her lover,
because therein lies a glimpse of the eternity our hearts were made to
contain.

But this kind of love is rare and priceless. All the wealth of the
world cannot purchase such love, as Solomon would soon learn. If "all
the wealth of his house" were offered, the Shulamite said, it would be
scorned.

LISTEN

Before we leave the *Song of Solomon* and delve into Solomon's wisdom, let's spend some time back in the garden where Solomon's love story began, and listen to what God has to say to us, His beloved:

LISTEN TO HIS WORDS

You can listen to God's love song to you by reading the *Song of Solomon* out loud. Or, if you're married, ask your spouse to read to you. Listen to the words of chapter four, verses 1–7. Pay close attention to their meaning, and think to yourself, "This is how the Lord sees me." This is His love song to us, His children.

"Behold, you are fair, my love!" he says. *"Behold you are fair! You have dove's eyes behind your veil. Your hair is like a flock of goats, going down from Mount Gilead"* (Song 4:1).

When I first pictured Solomon saying this to his Shulamite girl, I thought, well, "dove's eyes" isn't a bad start. The dove symbolized peace, tranquility, and quiet beauty. Not bad.

But then I tried the next line on Vicki: *"Your hair is like a flock of goats ... "* Something got lost in the translation. It didn't quite have the desired affect.

But in the cultural context of this shepherd girl, he adorned her with praise, because a flock of goats represented bountiful prosperity. By the time he finished the entire *Song* he had praised her from the top of her head to her beautiful feet (7:1), telling her how he loved and treasured her.

Do you believe—I mean truly believe—that the Lord loves you? Do you comprehend His passion for you and His desire to bless you? At first, the Shulamite shied away. When he pursued her, she answered,

"Do not look upon me, ... " She felt unworthy of his love.

No one is *worthy* of being loved by a holy God who also happens to be the King of the Universe, the Master of all Creation. But He still asks us to accept His love, to allow Him to bless us. While we see ourselves as wretched and sinful, He looks upon us and says, "But I have washed away that sin and wretchedness with My blood ... Behold, you are fair ..."

I've often chuckled over Mark Twain's words: "It ain't those parts of the Bible that I can't understand that bother me, it is the parts that I do understand."

What bothers me is when someone reads the Bible and misses the greatest truth of all—that God's Word is a love story, written for us in order to woo us into His kingdom. As Søren Kierkegaard said, "When you read God's Word, you must constantly be saying to yourself, 'it is talking to me and about me.' " God's Word is personal, life-changing, and yes, speaking directly to each of us.

LISTEN TO HIS HEART

Napoleon Bonaparte, the young military genius who emerged after the French Revolution in 1799, commanded fierce loyalty among his men. He wanted to instill in his soldiers "feu sacre"—sacred fire. He pushed them to serve with complete devotion, knowing that their only chance of victory was total commitment and a heart on fire for the cause.

Do you believe that God's heart burns with a sacred fire for us? In literature, the heart is defined as the "seat of affection." God's Word reveals where His affections lie. Read the next few verses and see His heart for us:

> Until the day breaks, and the shadows flee away, I will go my
> way to the mountain of myrrh and to the hill of frankincense.

You are all fair, my love ... Come with me from Lebanon, my spouse, ... Look from the top of Amana, from the top of Senir and Hermon, from the lions' dens, from the mountains of the leopards. You have ravished my heart.

—Song 4:6–9

Mount Senir, Mount Hermon, the mountain of myrrh, the mountains of leopards ... Solomon wants to take his beloved to the mountaintops, to the top of the world!

Mountains in the Bible represent places of privilege, beauty, and our spiritual journeys. God longs to take each of us by the hand and lead us up, above the wasteland and barrenness of this earthly life.

God planted the Garden of Eden on a mountaintop. He crowned his Creation with a beautiful home for his beloved Adam and Eve. Then they sinned and were banished. Translation: We left the Garden Paradise, stumbled down the mountain, and found ourselves in the howling wilderness, a barren land, blighted by fear, loneliness, and the ever-present specter of death. From Genesis to Revelation, the story of redemption is of God taking us from the lowlands back up to the mountain of paradise.

Over and over, throughout the Bible, God led His people to mountaintops: Abraham to Mount Moriah; Elijah to Mount Carmel; Moses to Mount Sinai. The children of Israel to Mount Zion; finally, Jesus to the Mount of Olives.

God wants to take each of us hiking up the mountain. Unfortunately, some people don't want to go. They hold back, timid and afraid to trust the Shepherd.

Personally, my whole life and ministry seemed to start when God said to me, "Son, walk with Me; I'm taking you to the mountaintops.

I want to reveal Myself to you, and I want to take as many people as I can with Me. I'm going to do everything I can to get you there quickly and safely, to raise your sights, lift your vision, and help you see from the top."

Are you willing to follow the Shepherd?

LISTEN TO HIS LOVE

"There is a land of the living and a land of the dead and the bridge is love, the only survival, the only meaning," wrote Thornton Wilder in *The Bridge of San Luis Rey*.

Mr. Wilder was right. There is a place to be alive, and a place to be emotionally and spiritually dead. There is life inside the garden of the Lord, and there is "life" outside where the world is cold, indifferent, and ignorant of love. Fortunately for us, God provided the bridge— Himself. When Jesus said, *"I am the way, the truth, and the life"* (John 14:6), He meant, "I am the bridge to get back to the Garden, back to the place of life."

"A garden enclosed is my sister, my spouse, a spring shut up, a fountain sealed. Your plants are an orchard of pomegranates with pleasant fruits," said Solomon to his beloved (4:12–13). He compared her to a garden, just as the Lord looks at your soul as a garden in need of tending and watering. After the seed of the Gospel is planted, God nourishes you with His living water, the Holy Spirit. He feeds you with the food of His Word. He prunes you and one day will send His holy fire to burn away the weeds, leaving only the best fruit.

Remember how God walked with Adam and Eve in the Garden? Close your eyes for a moment and picture your life as a fruit tree or a vine. Meditate on Psalm 1: *"Blessed is the man* [or woman] *who … shall be like a tree planted by the rivers of water, … "* (1,3).

How deep are your roots? Are they wide, but shallow? Will they stand through storms? Will they hold you when the ground is slipping away beneath you?

How are your branches? How far do they reach? Are the leaves supple and shining, full of the sap of life? Do they bear fruit? Good fruit like love, joy, peace, longsuffering, kindness, goodness, faithfulness, gentleness, self-control? Or are they dried up, easily broken, and full of pests?

Jesus said,

> I am the true vine, and my Father is the gardener. He cuts off every branch in me that bears no fruit, while every branch that does bear fruit he prunes so that it will be even more fruitful ... I am the vine; you are the branches. If a man remains in me and I in him, he will bear much fruit; apart from me you can do nothing.
>
> —John 15:1,5 NIV

ARE YOU SEALED?

Solomon described his beloved as *"a garden enclosed ... a spring shut up, a fountain **sealed** ... "* (4:12, emphasis added). Later, she responded by saying, *"Set me as a **seal** upon your heart, as a **seal** upon your arm"* (8:6, emphasis added). In the New Testament, in Paul's letters to the Ephesians and the Corinthians, he describes believers as being "sealed" with the Holy Spirit.

What does it mean to be "sealed"?

Both Corinth and Ephesus were lumbering centers during Paul's time. Logs were floated in from the Black Sea into their harbors, where builders would send their men to look them over. They made their selection, put down their deposits, then cut a certain kind of wedge into each log they had purchased. This was called the seal. The logs might wait in the harbor for many weeks, tossed about by various weather conditions, or be sent down the river to different destinations. But when the owners came to claim them, there was no mistaking which logs belonged to whom.

When Paul told the believers of these two logging towns that God had sealed them and that they were sealed with the Holy Spirit, they had a clear picture of what he meant. Though we are tossed about by the waters of life, like those logs, when the appointed time comes, our Lord will pick each of us out and claim us as His own, for we have been sealed.

When the Shulamite girl implored Solomon, *"Set me as a seal upon your heart ... upon your arm,"* he too knew what she meant: "Mark me as your own. Now that I have your vows verbally, seal me, wrap me, embrace me, encompass me, surround me, be with me, never leave me."

In ancient Israel, a seal showed ownership of a person's valued possessions. The Shulamite is asking to be her lover's most valued possession. *"Set me as a seal upon your heart,"* she said, indicating her influence over his heart and thoughts. And, *"as a seal upon your arm,"* referring to his actions.

"A fountain sealed" also carried a significant cultural implication. In the dry, desert land of the Middle East, pure water is a precious commodity. In Solomon's time, finding water was like striking gold. Even today, the battle over water rights is merely a continuation of centuries of fighting between Israel and Jordan. Upon finding a well or fountain, landowners quickly built a wall, sealed the fountain, and protected it under lock and key. Only the owner kept the key to the fountain.

In a world full of thorns, thistles, and dry wilderness, the Lord sees us as a precious fountain, one that can bless and refresh others, but also needs to be jealously guarded and protected from those who would misuse and abuse us.

Solomon was describing his beloved as a life-giving fountain that he desired to protect and cherish. He saw her as a garden of rich delights, fruit-bearing, life-giving, a recipient of his sacrificial love.

So God looks upon us. We are precious to Him. In a world where love has grown cold or is missing altogether, where ideals get trampled upon, where hearts are broken, God has reserved a place in His garden for each of us, if we will just accept it, where we can hear our name called "Beloved."

Part Two
WISDOM

The greatest good is wisdom.

—Saint Augustine

Chapter Four
THE ART OF LIVING

*U*NDER *the blossoming almond tree, Solomon paused to breathe in the fragrances playing in the cool breeze. He could feel the warmth of spring encroaching on winter's cold, awakening the earliest buds of his garden.*

People were waiting to see him. Good people. They came to him for advice, and he gladly shared it, still thankful for the gift. Wisdom.

He smiled. Of course Wisdom is a she. What else would something so inspiring be? A beautiful woman, calling him every day, desiring to share her most intimate secrets ...

The moss carpet under the tree looked richly inviting in the shaft of light trickling through the branches. He sat for a while, glad he had ordered his gardeners to line the walkways with spikenard, calamus, saffron, cinnamon ... the fragrances reminded him of the vineyard gardens in Ephraim. Nice, he thought, hoping the world could wait, as he closed his eyes.

She called to him, her voice floating down from the city gates on the hill. A vision of her danced through his dreams; he watched her move around her beautiful house, preparing, creating, laying out an elaborate feast.

"Listen," she said, "For I will speak to you of excellent things, and from the opening of my lips will come right things."

She slaughtered her meat, she mixed her wine, she furnished her tables, she sent out her maidens, she cried from the highest places of the city, "Whoever is simple, let him turn in here! He who lacks understanding ... come eat of my bread, drink of my wine ... forsake foolishness—and live!"

Solomon knew her name—Wisdom. He had met her long ago, in Gibeon. He could feel her wooing him, drawing him closer. It was foolish to resist. He followed her voice until he came face to face with a beautiful lady holding out her arms, a lover, a teacher, a friend—everything he needed to complete his life. Despite his own wealth and power, he realized he had come face to face with genuine treasure.

"I am understanding and I have strength," she assured him. "By me kings reign and rulers decree justice. By me princes rule, as well as nobles and judges."

He was the most powerful ruler in the known world, but she had his attention. Her claims intrigued him.

"Are you only the friend of the rich and powerful?" he asked.

"I love those who love me, and I am available to all who diligently seek me," she answered, gesturing toward her abundant treasures. "Riches and honor are with me.

"Ah! My fruit is better than gold—even fine gold and silver ... I travel the way of righteousness, in the midst of the path of justice, and I cause those who love me, who follow me, to inherit wealth and to fill their lives with treasure."

Solomon's storehouses overflowed with treasures, but they paled into meaningless baubles compared to the beauty of what she offered.

But wait, he thought. Who are you? Where did you come from? How do I know you are real?

"The Lord brought me forth as the first of His works," she answered. "I was appointed from eternity, from the beginning, before the world began, when there were no oceans. I was given birth when there were no springs abounding with water; before the mountains were settled into place, before the hills, I was given birth . . .

"I was there when He set the heavens in place, when He marked out the horizon on the face of the deep, when He established the clouds above, and fixed securely the fountains of the deep, when He gave the sea its boundaries and marked the foundations of the earth . . .

"Then I was the craftsman at His side. I was filled with delight day after day, rejoicing in His whole world and delighting in mankind."

On and on, she soothed him with her words, instructing and reproving, teaching him the art of living. "Blessed are those who keep my ways," she said, "For whoever finds me finds life and favor with the Lord."

How could he resist? How could he not stay with her, in her home, committed forever? Not since that night in Gibeon had he felt so spiritually strengthened. He recognized her as God's gift.

Wisdom had already touched his soul, enabling him to rule with compassion. His keen mind could examine the world with purpose and insight—and now he saw a vision of the future, when his nation would prosper under his leadership as it never had before.

The spring day's fragrances wafting through his dreams suddenly shifted, stirred by a cold wind. Even in this quiet repose under the almond tree, Solomon's body turned slightly as he heard another call, another voice, down another fork in the road.

A different woman sat at a different door, luring passersby into her home—appealing to those on their way to Wisdom's house. She also sat at the high places of the city, equally prominent, and in her own dark way, equally enticing.

"Whoever is simple," she says slyly, "let him turn here. Whoever lacks understanding, stolen bread is sweet. I have perfumed my bed with myrrh and cinnamon, and spread it with tapestry … come, let us take our fill of love, for my husband is not home."

Once again, Solomon saw a glimpse of his future, wrestling with these two voices all his life. He desired wisdom, but also saw detours ahead and he feared he would be pulled more than once into their dark paths.

The other one can seduce, he reminded himself, shaking off the dream, and opening his eyes to his garden again. Before he rose to go back to his court, one last warning pressed through his thoughts and he vowed to write it down as a reminder to himself and his future children. "Don't stray down her paths, for her house is the way to hell, descending into chambers of death."[15]

§

A WILD HORSE

"A man in a passion rides a wild horse," said Benjamin Franklin.

I admire the beauty, strength, and unbridled passion of a wild horse. I think there's something in all of us that wants to be like that. At least I hope so.

No one wants to live life with a weak, defeated, too-tame attitude. Then all the adventure is gone! The zest is missing! It's important that your spirit, your passion, your strength, and your desire to live and run the race are not broken. A spirit broken in the wrong way leaves you with no desire to run the race—to live—at all.

On the other hand, an unbridled horse is of little use. It can even be dangerous. So how do we keep the fire alive without crushing the spirit? How do we live with total abandon and joy without hurting those we love or being insensitive to others? How do we live with passion yet not be carried away on a wild horse?

Solomon gave us the answer when he wrote, in an urgent tone, *"Get wisdom!"* In his famous book of *Proverbs*, we are actually commanded to go find wisdom. I can think of nowhere else in the Bible where we are told to go get a godly virtue. Obviously, God has every intention of making it available.

That's Solomon's point. Wisdom is waiting, imploring, pleading, even enticing us to come to her. So passionately does Solomon want us to understand how real and vital is the wisdom he knows, that he likens this virtue to something he understands quite well—the love of a woman.

Our English word "wisdom" is translated in the Hebrew language as *chakam*, which means "skilled." Author Ron Jenson says, "To be wise is to be a craftsman at living, an artisan of life."[16]

An "artisan of life" sounds so satisfying and accomplished, doesn't it? But wisdom is not just an acquired accumulation of knowledge and wise sayings. No, it is a deeper, more substantial, and almost tangible attribute—like a person with whom we can have a relationship, according to Solomon, but not a common or prudent relationship. Wisdom waits for us with open arms, longing for our hearts to receive her, to allow her to shape and guide our lives.

Is there anything in your life that you care so deeply about that you can't stop thinking about it? Do you ever lay awake at night wondering how you are going to put this idea into action? A longing to write, a desire to be a better parent, a need to right a social injustice, to teach children, or to reach out to neighbors or comfort the sick … the list is as endless as the number of people who live on this earth. History proves that these passions of the heart can be used constructively—or destructively.

Wisdom is a manifestation of God's love, which helps us *guide* our passions, and then *matures* our passions into action.

More Passion, Please

Some friends and I often eat lunch at a restaurant that serves "passion" ice tea. We like to joke about ordering tea "with more passion, please."

Isn't that how we are about most things? We want to do our jobs well, and see our gifts blossom. But it can all begin to feel so boring if everything becomes too structured, safe—and tamed.

That's where wisdom and passion work, not to balance each other out, but to enhance the best qualities of each. Wisdom is a paradox. Readily available, but not easy to come by, it is both a gift and a learning process—something you can pray for, yet neglect to use.

Something you can study but fail to practice. As the subject of sacred and secular books, and the goal of countless individuals, corporations, and governments, wisdom has been personified, exalted, sought after, and analyzed. It is simplicity itself, yet profoundly mystical. It flows from the mouths of babes, yet takes a lifetime to realize.

Before a craftsman can put his skill to use, or an accomplished artist breathe life into her talents, each must be ignited to action by a *passion* for seeing those skills and gifts brought to fruition. So it is with life. We can't practice the art of living without a passion for living.

Our responsibility in all this is to *receive* what God is offering us, and to *pray* for teachable hearts, so that we can allow our passions to reach their potential and ensure godly wisdom will govern our passions.

TEACHABLE HEARTS

The Greeks used an interesting word to describe the taming of a wild and dangerous horse: meekness. The objective was to break the horse's will, to capture that unbridled energy, but never to break its *spirit*.

Using this same word, Jesus said a curious thing to His followers: *"The meek shall inherit the earth"* (Matthew 5:5). This isn't exactly what His friends had in mind when they pictured the conquering Messiah freeing them from oppression.

Picture a majestic, black stallion caught out on the range and corralled. As it paws the ground and breathes hot breath through flared nostrils, you can tell how restless and anxious it is to escape.

You can't get near it, but you love it. It is powerful and charged with energy and reminds you of the horses who bore the Knights of the Round Table, princes and princesses in fairy tales, and the cowboy heroes of the Wild West.

But a horse with unbridled passion and a will of its own is of no use to its master—and neither is one with a broken spirit. It takes great skill to break a horse's will without destroying its spirit. A horse with no spirit also has no desire, no stamina, and no readiness to go into battle with its master. You want it to have every ounce of its strength and vigor, but the horse left alone is dangerous. A horse, however, that has learned to respond to its master's every signal, nudge, and nuance is a treasure that can be encouraged to run to its full potential.

This is what wisdom is all about—the guide that directs and matures our passions without breaking our spirits.

A teenage girl confronted her mother with some harsh truths:

"I don't want to be like you," she said. "All I've heard my whole life is that you wanted to leave this place, move, and live somewhere else. But you never did it. Well, I'm leaving. I won't end up like you."

It's true, the mother thought. She had spent most of her adult life wanting to be somewhere else, doing something different. Her husband's work and family matters kept them in the same small, rural town year after year. Her resentment grew until she began to hate their life with a deadly passion. She deadened her fear of being stuck in mediocrity with alcohol. Guilt ate away at her faith and she began to avoid the intimacy she once knew with the Lord. Her bitterness seeped into her children's lives and now they were throwing it back at her.

"If I had been wiser, …" she confided to a friend.

"Yeah, I know. It's too bad you didn't move a long time ago."

"No," she said. "I wish I had allowed God to bless me. I wish I had never forgotten His love. I wish I had learned to be content … I should've practiced what I preach to my kids—you know, about

trusting the Lord. I knew we couldn't really move. Maybe someday …
but now, if I could do things differently, I would teach my children
that God's love is with us wherever we live—and I would be more
thankful for the life we've had."

This godly woman, a strong member of her church, knew all the
right things, but somehow the ability to put them into practice eluded
her. *But she possessed a teachable heart.* Wisdom, gleaned from years
of knowing God's Word, enabled her to change her attitude, and to
redeem the bitter years of regret. She began to put her education and
skills to work and to set a better example for her children. The tension
in her marriage eased as she let go of her resentment. She found peace
at last by fulfilling what she now believes is God's purpose for her life.
More importantly, she once again began to experience the love of God
guiding her life.

Wisdom, then, becomes a window through which we see God's love
and passion for us. When we comprehend His love, then we respond
with attitudes and actions that reflect wisdom working in our lives. But
sometimes the window is smudged and our vision is blurred.

WHERE DID WISDOM GO?

We are the most educated, experienced, and information-filled culture
that ever lived, yet I agree with T.S. Eliot's lament: "Where is the
wisdom we have lost in knowledge? Where is the knowledge we have
lost in information?"[17]

We are a culture in search of new experiences, looking for the next
event, the next adventure, the new knowledge—something, anything
that will feed our hungry souls. But experience that doesn't result in a
rekindled passion to know our Creator is just another event—another
bit of data logged into the computer called the brain. Books, counseling,

and even good spiritual teaching are capable of giving you insight, but sometimes they too are just another source of information.

Wisdom's song gets muted by a deluge of information. And yet, she can still be found gift-wrapped in a rich and multi-faceted book. His passion for Wisdom and her secrets compelled Solomon to write down what he learned in thousands of proverbs; 560 of those are recorded in the book of *Proverbs*.

This portion of Scripture is designed to teach us the art of living. Solomon stated right up front, like any good author, his purpose for writing:

> The proverbs of Solomon son of David, king of Israel: for attaining wisdom and discipline; for understanding words of insight; for acquiring a disciplined and prudent life, doing what is right and just and fair; for giving prudence to the simple, knowledge and discretion to the young—let the wise listen and add to their learning, and let the discerning get guidance.
>
> —Proverbs 1:1–5 NIV

That covers just about everyone. Wisdom prevents us from making poor choices, gives us the tools to get through difficult circumstances, provides the insight to learn from our mistakes, and helps us to discover purpose and direction for our lives. That's quite a gift.

Solomon concludes his introduction by observing that only *"fools despise wisdom"* (1:7).

BEGIN WITH GOD

A group of elementary school children described wisdom for me this way:

Brittany, age 10: "Wisdom is understanding things."

Elisabeth, age 9: "Wisdom is from God. He makes you wise."

Katie, age 13: "Wisdom helps you make wise decisions and use what God gives you."

Aaron, age 10: "Man thinks he is smart, but God's dumbest idea is smarter than man's greatest idea."

Some of them came up with proverbs of their own:

Rob, age 8: "To live an eternity, you must first die."

Uriah, age 6: "When I hit the ball, sometimes I don't hit a home run, but at least I hit the ball."

Josh, age 10: "A man who falls down on a skateboard and leaves is a failure, but he who tries again has not failed."

Audrey, age 9: "The wind can whisper enchanting things, but the Holy Spirit will whisper better."

Lastly, from little Kelsey and Julia, first graders: "Don't go near a dog because it might be a wolf," and "If you love God you will be happy."

Out of the mouths of babes.

A psychologist friend of mine said that wisdom means being able to line up the knowledge you've gained from experience with the emotions that are part of your personality, thereby positively influencing your subsequent actions. The formula is: *Cognitive knowledge + emotional insight + physical action = wisdom.*

Sounds good in theory, but awfully complicated—and incomplete.

Solomon summed up wisdom in one succinct phrase: *"The fear of the LORD is the beginning of knowledge, but fools despise wisdom ... "* (Proverbs 1:7).

Wisdom begins with God. If we condense all the words of wisdom ever written in the annals of great literature, they could be distilled down to that one thought.

Fear is translated from the Hebrew as "reverence or respect." The road map for our journey through life—God's Word—is designed to give us warnings, to point us in the right direction, to prevent us from falling, to help us make wise decisions, and to give us strength to overcome hardships. Out of respect for God and who He is, out of acknowledgment of His character and power, it is simply smart to follow God's Word. As Betsie ten Boom said, "The center of God's will is our only safety."[18]

In C.S. Lewis' *The Chronicles of Narnia,* Aslan the lion is an allegorical character who represents Jesus. When the children of Narnia heard of him the first time, Susan asked, "Is he—quite safe? I shall feel rather nervous about meeting a lion."

"That you will, dearie, and no mistake," said Mrs. Beaver, "if there's anyone who can appear before Aslan without their knees knocking, they're either braver than most or else just silly."[19]

I think that puts it nicely. The beginning of wisdom is to *fear* God because it is just plain silly not to.

"Trust in the LORD with all your heart," Solomon continued later. *"Lean not on your own understanding; in all your ways acknowledge Him, and He shall direct your paths"* (3:5–6). If living is truly an art, then we need to put our lives into the hands of the Master Artist.

How to Get Wisdom—the Short and Sweet Answer

Wisdom, believe it or not, can be immediately possessed—but it may require a lifetime to cultivate. James 1:5 promises straightforwardly,

"If any of you lacks wisdom, let him ask of God, who gives to all liberally and without reproach, and it will be given to him." That's how you get wisdom.

An Abundant Answer

Is it really that easy? Jesus said, *"What man is there among you who, if his son asks for bread, will give him a stone? Or if he asks for a fish, will he give him a serpent?"* (Matthew 7:9–10). So if you ask for wisdom from your heavenly Father, you can be sure that He will give it to you—just as He answered Solomon's request. Solomon received the one thing that ensured everything else he might desire. In fact, he got more than he asked for. *"Behold, I have done according to your words,"* the Lord said to him. *"I have given you a wise and understanding heart ... and I have also given you what you have not asked: both riches and honor"* (1 Kings 3:12–13).

James said that if we ask for wisdom, we will get it. Period. But he also wants us to understand the process. Look at verses 2 through 4 of James chapter 1: *"Consider it pure joy, my brothers, whenever you face trials of many kinds, because you know that the testing of your faith develops perseverance. Perseverance must finish its work so that you may be mature and complete"* (NIV).

Wisdom is like salvation. While God gives us the instant gift of salvation and eternal life the moment we ask, He also has a plan for maturing us in the faith. He allows time to "work out our own salvation with fear and trembling, for it is God who works in us ..." (see Philippians 2:12–13).

God not only gives us wisdom "liberally" and immediately, but He also develops wisdom in our lives through a maturing process that will most likely include trials and times of testing.

"WE'RE IN HIS HANDS"

The Delany sisters, Bessie and Sadie, each lived over one hundred years—that's a lot of accumulated wisdom! In their book, *The Delany Sisters' Book of Everyday Wisdom*, they wrote about their beloved "Papa," a former slave, who was elected the first black bishop of the Episcopal Church of America. In 1918 he was asked to be a guest preacher at a church in Raleigh, Virginia. His family considered the invitation a great honor, so all ten children and his wife attended. Even though Papa was the guest of honor, his family was sent to the back balcony. Bessie recalls, "They made us sit where the slaves had been made to sit. And then we were not given the privilege of Communion."

When the story appeared in the sisters' first book, they received a formal letter of apology from the congregation of that church. Bessie writes, "We were so touched that they apologized a full seventy-five years later. Now that's God's work."

Seventy-five years! Decades over which bitterness could have hardened these women's hearts. But something insulated them from such destructive emotions. Something motivated them to live free, productive lives, each following her passion. "We set aside time every day to talk to the Lord," Sadie wrote. "After all, He has to manage the whole world and He's never too busy for us!"

Bessie recalled, "When we walk into our house—whether we're coming back from a long trip or just from seeing our neighbors—the first thing we say is, 'Praise the Lord.' We do that to thank Him for watching over us."[20]

That story appears in their book under the heading, "We're in His Hands." These two black women, growing up in an era when that meant two strikes against them, could almost have been excused for resenting their circumstances. But Bessie and Sadie lived successfully and accomplished amazing things during their one hundred plus years on earth—a remarkable testimony of God's wisdom at work.

"Wisdom is better than rubies ..." says Proverbs 8:11.

William Webster (of dictionary fame) told about the time one of his young children mangled that verse to read, "Wisdom is better than rubbish." After being amused, he thought about it and said, "How true it is that all else is rubbish in comparison with true wisdom."[21]

Chapter Five
WHAT'S REAL?

THE HARLOT'S BABY

A sleepy stupor hung over her as she tried to crawl off her sleeping pallet. What woke her? Not noise or commotion. Stillness. It was too quiet. Nothing stirred or rustled; no soft breath warmed her face.

Trying to shake off the haze of wine and heavy sleep, she ran her hands across the small form lying under her blankets. Pausing for a moment, she pressed harder; then again. Fear began to cut through her confusion as she shook the little bundle, gently at first, then with a ferocious rhythm as if to drown out the fear pounding in her chest.

Breathing as quietly as her panic would allow, she finally stopped, realizing the futility. She needed to think. Soft moonlight filtered through door cracks, outlining another sleeping figure. She contemplated her friend, watching to see how soundly she slept. She heard the other baby's infant snores and a plan began to shape in her mind.

The sisterhood she shared with her roommate was one of necessity. Two women, whose trade had made them allies, needing a shelter to birth their babies. They had agreed to help each other, share a room, and provide some sort of companionship in a society where they were outcasts. The birth of a harlot's baby was of no consequence to anyone else.

She gathered her still infant in her arms, took one last look at the quiet, cold face, allowed herself a moment of sorrow, then laid the bundle next to her sleeping friend. Quickly she scooped up the other baby, shushed its wakening whimper by holding it to her breast, then curled back up into her thin blankets.

She laid quietly in the dark, waiting for the first signs of morning. As soon as she heard the town stirring, she hurried out into the wakening street to find a morning meal.

"My son is the living son!"

"No! The dead one is your son. My son is the living one!"

§§§

Solomon watched the two women approaching him, their bitter argument announcing their arrival. Looking carefully for clues to their dilemma, he quickly recognized their profession. Faded beauty, perhaps once genuine, now propped up by artifice, barely hid their tired and hardened countenances. He watched them berate each other, listening as their stories spilled out, each trying to talk louder and more convincingly than the other.

The infant in question hung, almost like a casual accessory, on one woman's arm, while she waved the other at her companion, punctuating her shouts and denials.

"O king," the childless one pleaded, "this is my son. She smothered her baby in the night. She took my son from my side, while your maidservant slept, and laid him in her bosom, and laid her dead child in my bosom."

"No!" the other cried again, "my son lives!"

Back and forth they argued. Solomon listened, contemplating how to provoke the truth from them.

"Bring me a sword." He stopped their debate with his command.

The court looked curious. They had yet to see Solomon put to such a test of judgment. Skeptical looks were exchanged.

"Bring me the living child and the dead child." The guards complied.

One mother looked curious; the other horrified; others were amused, assuming Solomon would be made the fool.

"Cut both children into two pieces. Each woman may have half the living child and half the dead one."

While the court stirred with ripples of laughter ("what do you expect from one so young?"), and nervous exchanges, the women scurried closer to Solomon.

"Fine," said one. "Start with mine," and she handed the bundled infant to a guard. Looking at the other woman, she spit out a whisper, "You can suffer the same torment I have."

"No! No! Spare the baby!" the other cried. "O my lord, give her the living child and by no means kill him." She collapsed at his feet, pleading for compassion, declaring herself to be content to see the child live, even with another mother.

The king understood. Their words proceeded from the truth of their passions. He turned to the guard and commanded, "Give this woman the living child. She is the mother."

Before he turned away, he looked toward the other woman,

saying, "It was not enough that you killed your own child. You chose to compound your wickedness by endeavoring to destroy your friend's child and cause her to suffer."

As Solomon walked away, a torrent of whispers and exclamations began to circulate through the court, out on the streets and beyond. Eager storytellers spread the news throughout the kingdom of the judgment and Solomon's sagacity in discerning the truth.

With that swift and canny judgment, Solomon had secured the respect of his court, and earned the right to dispense words of wisdom.[22]

§

With sword poised and ready to strike, Solomon intended to uncover the truth.

When the author of the book of Hebrews wrote centuries later, *"For the word of God is living and powerful, and sharper than any two-edged sword ... "* (4:12) did he have Solomon's sword in mind? *"It penetrates even to dividing soul and spirit, joint and marrow; it judges the thoughts and attitudes of the heart"* (4:12 NIV).

The inner life of a believer is an odd mixture of motivations, some spiritual, some selfish, as interwoven as the "joints and marrow" of our own bodies. Even when we aspire to good things, our motives are flawed.

The Hebrews attributed power to words. Once spoken, a word existed independently. It became more than the sound of vowels and consonants. Words went forth and did things. *"In the beginning God created the heavens and the earth. ... and God said, 'let there be light,' ... and there was light"* (Genesis 1:1,3 NIV).

The Word of God is living and full of energy. It possesses the power to expose the intentions of our hearts and to reveal what is motivated by the Spirit and what is not. *"Nothing in all creation is hidden from God's sight. Everything is uncovered and laid bare before the eyes of him to whom we must give account"* (Hebrews 4:13 NIV).

Anyone can read the Bible. Many do. But to experience the Word as the holy eyes of God—peering into our hearts, allowing Him to see our intentions and motivations—that's another thing altogether. Like the harlots, we may find ourselves exposed and naked before Him, defensive, desperate to avoid humiliation, dodging truth to the degree that we would allow a child to die rather than admit our spiritual poverty.

If only we could see how unnecessary all this pretense is! The embarrassing and humiliating reality we run from is the very thing Jesus said is a virtue! *"Blessed are the poor in spirit, for theirs is the kingdom of heaven"* (Matthew 5:3).

Remember how unworthy the Shulamite girl felt, cowering under the radiance of Solomon's countenance? *"Do not look upon me, because I am dark ... "* she lamented. She wanted to run, to fix herself up, to cover up the evidence of her hard life.

But he looked at her and saw none of that. *"Behold, you are fair, my love!"* he said. He saw only her beauty.

We can take off the masks. God loves us as we really are, behind our facades, because He sees the real us—the children He created to love and cherish. He sees us as His beloved. We can be real—if we can just figure out what real is.

REALITY IN AN UNREAL WORLD

Recently I underwent the new laser procedure on my eyes. It was miraculous! Once I was blind, but now I see! I was concerned, however, by the doctor's suggestion to deliberately fix my eyes to different strengths—one for close up, one for distance. He explained that in time, my brain would merge the two strengths together and I wouldn't be able to tell the difference.

Another doctor friend told me of studies where special contact lenses turn the subject's vision upside down. Within two weeks, the individual's brain adapts and turns everything right side up again. That's how easily our perception can be changed.

"Wisdom and truth will enter the very center of your being, filling your life with joy," Solomon once wrote (Proverbs 2:9–10 TLB).

Those who live with "wisdom and truth" at the very center of their beings are the true realists. The lie is that the world of sexual confusion, abandoned babies, substance abuse, wars, pain, and suffering is "real." This is not the world God intended for His children, but because we have to live in it every day, our perceptions tell us that this is reality.

When Jesus walked on the earth, those who walked with Him were amazed by the miracles He performed. The supernatural world had broken into their lives, astounding them, opening their eyes to new possibilities, to new ways of thinking. Miracles were regarded then, as they are now, as a temporary suspension of reality. But the opposite is actually true. The miracles of Jesus were moments of reality breaking through into the unreal world.

What seems miraculous and unnatural to us is normal for the kingdom of God! Solomon wrote in his later years that God *"put eternity"* in our hearts (Ecclesiastes 3:11). We are *supposed* to live with an understanding of His eternal kingdom and to experience His supernatural power.

Reality is obscured every single day, every time we reject or deny truth. When our perceptions are rooted in God's Word and *His* perception of who we are, we are living according to the truth. When our vision gets skewed and we look at life without God's perspective, then we start seeing the events and circumstances of our lives through a deceptive prism—and after a while all the junk around us begins to look "normal."

God put Adam and Eve upon the earth in the real world He intended for them—Paradise. The day they chose to disobey Him, believing the lie Satan dangled in front of them *("You will not surely die ... you will be like God"* [Genesis 3:4–5]), was the day they chose to walk out of reality into the morass of unreality, and sin and confusion have plagued the human race ever since.

The two harlots stood before Solomon as examples of reality obscured. Their profession spoke volumes about their perception of life. The unreal world rationalizes harmful lifestyles by saying, "I need to support myself," or "I need to make money," or "This is the only life I know," etc., etc.

Reality is that God already promised to care for His children. But when we're impatient and leave His kingdom in search of provisions, we usually end up doing something that will harm us. When we enter into a relationship of trust with the Lord, however, then we step back into the real world. We allow reality to be manifested by what will seem like miracles to others, but which we come to recognize as "normal" in the kingdom of God.

I stopped one day to meditate on a familiar verse. Jesus said, *"You shall know the truth, and the truth shall make you free"* (John 8:32). Why? Why would the truth *make* us free? Knowing the truth is hard. Sometimes the truth feels like a burden. Remember that line spoken by Jack Nicholson in the movie *A Few Good Men:* "You can't handle the truth!'"? We can't handle the truth when the only truth we see is sin and hurt and heartache! But Jesus wants us to know truth as it is defined in the kingdom of God. *"Seek first the kingdom of God,"* He said (Matthew 6:33). *"Thy Kingdom come. Thy will be done,"* He prayed (Matthew 6: 10 KJV). Get your priorities in order. First the kingdom. Reality. Then God's will and His blessings will be poured out upon you as you live in His kingdom.

Every day, every one of us needs to make a conscious decision to meditate on God's Word and to choose to live in the "real" world.

Truth Defines Us

> For he endured, as seeing him who is invisible.
>
> —Hebrews 11:27 KJV

The truth of who we are in God's eyes is crucial to defining our lives. When we recognize the truth and choose to follow, it's not usually the easy way—but it will always be the most fulfilling way. As I said earlier, though Jesus promised *"the truth shall make you free,"* He didn't say that the truth would be easy—but He did make it the criteria for freedom.

Again and again, people of faith have been brought to moments of truth, only to discover that in facing truth, three issues are at stake: their *identities*, their *priorities*, and the *challenges* they will face.

Identity: Who Am I?

Remember the story of the infant Moses, born into a perilous political situation? His mother hid him for three months, then sealed him in a waterproof basket and sent him down the river, praying that his life would be spared.

Imagine, after growing up in luxury, wealth, and power what he must have felt when he realized that his true identity lay with an oppressed and enslaved people. Moses faced an identity crisis: born a Hebrew, yet reared as an Egyptian prince. We know that he chose his own people, but did he make that noble decision all on his own? I don't believe so.

God opened his eyes and his heart. When Moses saw an Egyptian beating a Hebrew slave, the truth so overwhelmed him that he reacted violently. *"He looked this way and that way,"* the Bible tells us, *"and when he saw no one, he killed the Egyptian and hid him in the sand"* (Exodus 2:12). Realizing he could be punished with death, Moses fled to the wilderness.

The book of Hebrews tells us that, *"By faith Moses … refused to be called the son of Pharaoh's daughter, choosing rather to suffer affliction with the people of God than to enjoy the passing pleasures of sin"* (Hebrews 11: 24–25).

Faith opened Moses' eyes to the truth and his heart responded. But he hardly behaved like a hero. By faith, Moses identified with his people, but beyond that, he didn't really know what to do—which is exactly where God wanted him. He allowed Moses to be stuck out in the desert for forty years; meanwhile Pharaoh died, and his successor increased the oppression of his people. Moses raised a family, grew old, and no doubt wondered many times what his time in Egypt was all about.

Until one day, God appeared to him in a burning bush. A consuming fire that didn't consume—the flame of God's presence, His passion, and now His purposes, revealed to Moses after all these years.

By *faith*, Moses chose to see the truth of his own identity—and God did the rest.

PRIORITY

Once Moses recognized the truth of his identity, *"he regarded disgrace for the sake of Christ as of greater value than the treasures of Egypt, because he was looking ahead to his reward"* (Hebrews 4:26). Moses began to see life through God's eyes. He began to understand what he was supposed to be looking for. Not riches or power or prestige. The ultimate reward is to be in God's presence, doing God's will.

Moses made a choice—then God adjusted his lifestyle. Forty years in the desert can do that! The value system Moses developed can be outlined like this:

§   *GOD'S PURPOSE IS MORE IMPORTANT THAN POPULARITY*

Moses learned to live for an audience of one—the Lord. He let go of his potential political power in Egypt, and later, as the Israelites' leader, he often had to make unpopular decisions (remember how the people grumbled?). He lived to please God.

§   *PEOPLE ARE MORE VALUABLE THAN PLEASURE*

Do you realize the pleasures and creature comforts Moses could have had in Egypt—at the expense of his own people? Once he saw the truth, he could no longer accept his people's oppression.

§   *GOD'S PEACE IS MORE VALUABLE THAN POSSESSIONS*

All the treasures in Egypt brought Moses no peace. He had watched an entire people group being brutalized to provide Pharaoh with wealth and luxury.

§   *GOD'S PASSION IS MORE VALUABLE THAN WORLDLY POWER*

Moses learned that the wilderness held more for him than Pharaoh's court, because there in the desert, he met the living God.

THE CHALLENGE

The challenge God lays before each of us is also an invitation. Are we willing to leave what we think is reality for the sake of knowing Him? "Truth is a kingdom which belongs to those who give themselves to it, lead where it may, cost what it will, use or not use,"[23] wrote Ralph Sockman.

By faith, Moses left Egypt, and endured years of failure in the wilderness. Yet, he persevered *"as seeing Him who is invisible"* (Hebrews 11:27).

He could have given up, decided it was too much—this God stuff. After all, a pretty big responsibility was being laid on him. But Moses persevered, not because he was such a strong, disciplined person, but rather *because he knew the passion of God.*

How long are you willing to wait for the passions of your heart to be ignited into God's holy purposes? Moses waited in the desert for forty years, tending sheep, asking himself many times, I'm sure, what he was doing there and why he had walked away from everything he had always known.

Then one day a voice spoke to him from a burning bush, and Moses knew the wait had been worthwhile.

When Moses entered the tabernacle, Exodus 33:11 tells us, *"the LORD spoke to Moses face to face, as a man speaks to his friend."* Moses became a friend of God.

Are you ready to see a burning bush? Seeing life through God's eyes might mean an exile in the wilderness. It may mean willingly being severed from the outward luxury of this world. But the reward is to enter into His transcendent presence, to be consumed by His love, to be made alive by His passion for you—and to realize that He sees you as someone with a grand purpose in life.

This is exactly where we will next meet Solomon—getting ready to fulfill a grand purpose.

Chapter Six
A DWELLING PLACE FOR GOD

THE HOUSE KING SOLOMON BUILT

*F*IRE *swept down, as if on a thunderbolt, rushing with violence to lick up the slain sheep and bulls lain across the altar. Smoke rose instantly, as the animals were consumed in a brilliant burst of heat. Soon, the hot fury was tempered by a gentle, sweet, and heavy cloud, which hung in the air, soothing and filling out the interior of the temple.*

The priests drew back, even though Solomon remained on his knees, hands outstretched above him. He didn't want to move. Not yet.

He heard the voices of the people respond to the display of power. Joy and wonder echoed through their song; he sensed their collective bowing. But for this moment, he wanted to rest, just as he knew that for this short breath in eternity, the glory of God rested; all the power and magnificence of heaven poured into this sanctuary, this house that Solomon had labored over for seven years. He felt God's pleasure and acceptance as he thanked the Lord for this moment, for allowing him to build the temple.

He had relished every minute.

"Gold for the things of gold, silver for the things of silver …" Daily, Solomon had pored over lists of materials. Silver and gold were there in abundance. David had set up a rich treasury for the Lord's temple.

He had rolled out the scrolls for the master builders, filled with detailed instructions: Specific measurements, specific weights for everything from lampstands, tables, golden bowls, the incense altar, and of course the golden cherubim whose wingspans would overshadow the actual ark, shielding the Holy of Holies with their beauty.

Seventy thousand workmen, eighty thousand quarry men, plus another thirty-six hundred overseers were recruited. Huram, the master craftsman, had arrived, a gift from King Hiram of Tyre, to orchestrate the entire project. The timber, hewn from the cedars of Lebanon, could be seen bobbing on the horizon, arriving in massive convoys of rafts by sea.

Four hundred eighty years had passed since his people escaped their bondage in Egypt. Four years into his reign, Solomon prepared to build a place of worship for them, one that would truly glorify God and give his people a place of sanctuary. He studied the plans with excitement, carried them around with him, and threw himself into the work.

For seven years, Mount Moriah remained a beehive of activity. From the moment the foundation was laid (sixty cubits long and twenty cubits wide) Solomon watched every detail being placed exactly as David's plans instructed. He couldn't stay away. Even with accomplished men supervising the project, Solomon spoke often with Huram, and gave personal instructions for the placements of the gold, the precious stones, and carved wood. He helped fashion the gold overlays, measured the wingspans of the cherubim, instructed the workers exactly how the wreaths of precious metal chainwork would top the massive pillars. He fingered the fine linens of blue and purple and crimson, designed the cherubim images to be woven into the fabric, and then watched as the veil that would cover the inner sanctuary was hung. He closed off the Most Holy Place with doors of gold, and waited for the day when the ark of the covenant would have a worthy home.

Seven swift years. They passed too quickly. The temple may have been David's legacy, but it was Solomon's crowning achievement. He knew the Lord was pleased, and his heart was at peace.

Earlier that morning, he had stood on the porch, surrounded by all the heads of the tribes of Israel, and the elders of the families. The crisp, autumn morning was spiced by rich incense, burning in immense quantities in honor of the great day. The traditional Feast of Tabernacles promised to be even greater this year.

Solomon had watched the streets of Jerusalem, which were trembling with anticipation. Priests who had carefully proceeded up the winding and crowded streets shouldered the ark of the covenant, held by poles which passed through rings on the sides of the sacred box. The people pressed in, eager to be near, yet cautious.

Would God be pleased? Would His glory be manifested?

As the procession drew closer, the king heard unrestrained singing and saw movements on the horizon as the crowd danced in exultation, just as his father David had danced. "You are holy, who inhabit the praises of Israel," he whispered softly, fervently praying that the Lord would dwell among His people.

It had been so long, he reflected, hundreds of years. The ancient ones, Adam and Eve, knew God in all His glory. Jehovah had walked and talked with them in the Garden in the cool of day. When they brought evil into the world, God banished them from Paradise and withdrew His glory. Solomon once knew the paradise of a garden, long ago when he fell in love. He grieved for the loss.

Noah witnessed the horror of a flood covering the whole earth, surpassed only by the wickedness and depravity God chose to eliminate. All flesh died, all who breathed, the scrolls taught him. Then a flash of God's glory burst forth in a multi-colored ray of light. The rainbow ... a prism of the glory, a fractured piece of heaven and a promise of greater things to come.

Abraham encountered God's glory when he stood, knife poised, and heard the Angel command him to spare Isaac. Abraham must have trembled at that voice that could change death to life in an instant. Solomon knew that it was on this very site, where the new temple stood, that Abraham had offered Isaac in faith to the Lord.

Moses actually saw the backside of God's glory! The Shekinah, his teachers called it. He pictured Moses, standing before a burning bush that wouldn't burn; seeing light that wasn't light; hiding in the cleft of a rock, protected just enough to guard his life against the power that no mortal

can look upon and live. Moses' face lit up as he ran down the
mountain, glowing, trying to hold on to the glory by covering
his countenance with a veil.

But even Moses could not contain the Shekinah. So they
built the ark, a beautiful boxed sanctuary to carry the sacred
tablets and to provide a place for God to dwell among the
children of Israel.

As if God could be contained! Not in the ark, the tabernacle,
nor even in this temple! Solomon reached higher, stretching his
arms as far as they could reach, exulting in God's answer to his
prayer:

"Arise, O LORD God, to Your resting place, You and the ark
of Your strength. Let Your priests ... be clothed with salvation
and Your saints rejoice in goodness. O LORD, do not turn Your
face away from Your anointed; remember the mercies of Your
servant David."

And with that, fire came down, and glory filled the
temple.[24]

§

GLORY FILLS THE TEMPLE—AND YOUR LIFE

It is a crisp autumn day as I write this—much like the day Solomon
dedicated the temple. The time of year when costumed children come
to your door looking for candy and someone pulls out the *Legend of
Sleepy Hollow,* the story of poor Ichabod Crane.

As a boy I didn't know the significance of Ichabod's name, but as a
young Bible student I discovered its meaning in the book of 1 Samuel:
Ichabod means "the glory of the Lord has departed," and what remains

is godless, desolate—a vacuum for evil and disaster. Definitely a good, scary name.

Ichabod figuratively became a prominent character in the landscape of Israel's history. God withdrew His glory reluctantly in response to Israel's faithlessness. The temple, Solomon's masterpiece, would eventually be destroyed. Though Habakkuk the prophet proclaimed that the glory would return when the temple was rebuilt, the *Shekinah* never manifested itself again on such a national level. When the glory days of Solomon's reign ended, Israel soon forgot what it was like to experience the presence of God ... until one winter night, centuries later. While shepherds watched their flocks, the night sky suddenly lit up with a burst of light, accompanied by heavenly voices heralding the birth of the King! A tiny baby, lying quietly in an obscure manger, brought the glory of God back to dwell on the earth.

"The Word became flesh and dwelt among us, and we beheld His glory" (John 1:14a). (When was the last time you "beheld" the glory of God?) But it didn't stop there. Moses witnessed the burning bush, ablaze with fire that didn't consume; Jesus, however, called His disciples the branches of the new tree of life *("I am the vine, you are the branches ... ")*. He came to baptize us with fire, setting our hearts ablaze with the power of the Holy Spirit. We are the burning bushes of the church age!

On the Day of Pentecost, fire came down from heaven once again, only this time to rest upon the heads of the early church. Not like in Solomon's time when the fire consumed. No, this time they sacrificed the Lamb of God, Jesus, on the Cross. This fire was the glory of God reaching its ultimate destination: the human heart. This fire rode on the wings of the Holy Spirit, returning to empower His people with love and strength from on high.

God's passion for you will direct and guide your life, as long as you remember that the practical goal of realizing your life's purpose *must be preceded by experiencing the passion of God.* As you look at this relationship of passion to purpose, ask God to give you your own Day of Pentecost. Ask His Holy Spirit to come down and fill you with His glory, opening your eyes to the wonderful possibilities He has in store for you.

THE HAUNTING QUESTION

Os Guinness calls it "the haunting question." The question through which we filter so much of our life: Do I have a purpose? A calling? A reason to live? And if I do, how do I fulfill the central purpose of my life?

Fyodor Dostoevsky observed in *The Brothers Karamazov,* "For the secret of man's being is not only to live but to have something to live for. Without a stable conception of the object of life, man would not consent to go on living, and would rather destroy himself than remain on earth, …"[25] Not consent to go on living!? I can't imagine a more terrifying and desperate sentence with which to condemn a man.

Remember that childhood song, "Hide your light under a bushel— no! I'm gonna let it shine!"? God's glory is once again manifested on the earth, only this time, the temple is us! *"Do you not know that your body is the temple of the Holy Spirit?"* Paul wrote (1 Corinthians 6:19a).

To paraphrase the great preacher, John Wesley, "I allow myself to be set on fire by the Holy Spirit, then people come to watch me burn."

IS THERE A REASON FOR MY LIFE?

Romuald Waszkinel often searched in the mirror as a young man for some resemblance to his Polish parents. His life, filled with school, family, parties, music, and youthful carousing, sailed on fairly smooth waters—except for a vague undercurrent of questions without answers.

Once, a couple of drunks called him a Jewish orphan, but his mother, Emilia, dismissed them as foolish. "There is no need to listen to bad people," she assured him, and tried to push his confusion aside.

When he shocked his parents at the age of 17 by announcing his desire to be a priest, his father's profuse weeping and impassioned plea to reconsider dismayed him. Weeks later, the elderly man died of a heart attack. The future priest's faith temporarily wavered as he struggled through guilt and grief. But then an even stronger conviction took hold: "If my father was afraid I would be a bad priest, it was up to me to prove I could be a good one. My decision became irrevocable."

In the next few years, Waszkinel sensed a secret; his discomfort at the church's teaching about Jews led him to question the often-held belief that all Jews were bad, responsible for the murder of Jesus. The tears he saw in his mother's eyes whenever he read to her about the Jews (she was illiterate) prompted him to ask her one day, "Why are you crying? Am I Jewish?"

Emilia simply responded, "Don't I love you enough?"

Finally, his mother, hospitalized for cancer, revealed the truth—he was the son of Jewish parents, victims of the Holocaust. His father had been a well-known tailor. His mother, trapped in a ghetto being stormed by Nazi troops, contacted Emilia and begged her to take her infant son and save his life. When Emilia hesitated, the desperate mother said something eerily prophetic: "You believe in Jesus, and after all, [He] was a Jew. You have to save this Jewish baby because of who you believe in. And once he grows up, he will become a priest."

As he reconnected with the family of his father, Jakub Weksler, the priest discovered that some of his newfound Jewish relatives were angered by his devotion to Christianity. He says, however, "I never had a doubt. I know that Jesus saved me. He found me in a ghetto. He was my most wonderful Jew."

When he visited the former Nazi concentration camp of Majdanek, and walked among the Jewish school children who were being taught their history, Romuald Jakub Weksler-Waszkinel realized that God planned to use him as a bridge between two cultures. "I am in the middle," he says, "and I know that what is needed is contact, understanding, and love."

He continues to live his life and pursue his ministry with an even stronger conviction that God has a specific purpose for him, one that no human failing, hatred, or prejudice can thwart, as long as he follows the call God put in his heart. For Romuald Jakub Weksler-Waszkinel the haunting question has been answered.[26]

The great preacher Billy Sunday said, "More men fail through lack of purpose than lack of talent." Life gets boring as apathy and frustration set in when we don't quite know what to do with ourselves. Norman Mailer, always stretching for the largeness of life, wrote, "I don't think life is absurd. I think we are all here for a huge purpose. I think we shrink from the immensity of the purpose we are here for."[27]

We shrink from our purpose because we don't actually know what to do, or why we should do it, and we are afraid to try. Sometimes, we're not even sure we should bother.

But to not bother is to be "haunted" throughout our lives, looking for a reason to accept life, hoping for significance, yearning for fulfillment.

DISCOVERING MY PURPOSE RELIEVES STRESS

A phenomenal explosion of knowledge and information has impacted our culture, resulting in unlimited choices. We can't even buy a soda without deciding on diet, caffeine-free, cherry, classic, color, no-color. There used to be two choices—take it or leave it.

In a culture where two hundred new magazines a year are published and approximately two hundred new grocery items hit the stores every week, we are drowning in choices! No wonder young people have such a hard time deciding what to do, what school to attend, what career to follow, who to marry, when to marry, or if they should marry.

Jesus had a friend who seemed confused about what she should do with her time. *"One thing is needed,"* He said to Martha one day. She was troubled and worried, trying to juggle her household responsibilities with being a good hostess—while her sister, Mary, sat at His feet, appearing far too relaxed.

Martha's well-intentioned busyness did not impress the Lord. And, if she was tired and irritable because of it, I'm not sure how much anyone else appreciated her either. She was mad at her sister for just sitting there calmly at Jesus' feet, listening to His words. Imagine her surprise when she complained to Him and He took Mary's side! "She has chosen what is better, and it will not be taken away from her," He said (see John 10).

"Well, that's just great," you might think. "I wish I had all day to sit at Jesus' feet. Sure, it would be easy to be really spiritual, to know God so intimately. But in the meantime, who runs my business or my household? Who feeds the dog, mows the lawn, drives the kids, and pays the bills? I know what my purpose in life is—it's to get everything done every day that needs doing!"

If you're an adult who's "arrived," you're loaded down with responsibilities. If you're young (or old) and still trying to figure out what to do with your life, the myriad of options is confusing. The answer to all this is in Jesus' words: *"One thing is needed."*

As I grow older, I've learned that I can't do everything. I have been fortunate enough to fulfill many of my hopes and dreams, but I've also had to pass on a few. I know what God put a passion in my heart to do, and by responding to that passion, I'm discovering that ultimately my deepest desires are being fulfilled.

I may never play professional sports (one of my childhood dreams), but my desire to throw myself into something I believe in, with all the same dedication and zeal—and support my family—has been satisfied through a full-time ministry. I may never live out on a mission field in an exotic, foreign land, but my love for God's Word and my desire to teach are completely fulfilled every time I step up to a pulpit.

Being confused creates stress. The Bible reminds us that a *"double-minded man* [is] *unstable in all his ways"* (James 1:8). It's stressful to be uncertain about what to do with your life.

When you take the time to sit at the Lord's feet, your purpose will become clearer. A purpose frees you up to be more creative, more adventurous, and more passionate about what you do, because you know where you're going and whom you're following.

Living with Purpose Will Give Me Strength

People who live without a motivating passion are usually tired and lacking in inspiration. It's hard to drag yourself out of bed every day if you have no reason to. Living with a God-inspired purpose gives you the motivation each morning to "take on the day."

I believe that when God calls us, He plants a passion deep in our hearts that so moves us, we cannot help but act. Os Guinness defines God's call this way: "Calling is the truth that God calls us to himself so decisively that everything we are, everything we do, and everything we have is invested with a special devotion, dynamism, and direction lived out as a response to his summons and service."[28]

When Solomon knew what he was called to do and did it, he lived gloriously. However, Josephus the historian described the end of Solomon's life this way: "He died ingloriously."

I may be jumping ahead here, but most of you know that somehow along the way, Solomon began to meander all over the spiritual and philosophical landscape. His early years flourished with wisdom. A tangible purpose motivated him: to honor the Lord and to build the temple. His reign ushered Israel into her Golden Age. The temple, the kingdom, it was all glorious—until Solomon lost sight of his purpose. He acquired treasures and power. He basked in the approval of men and past accomplishments, but forgot his own exhortation the day he dedicated the temple: *Let your heart be loyal to the LORD our God, to walk in His statutes and keep His commandments, ...* " (1 Kings 8:61).

Influenced by foreign wives, Solomon allowed himself to worship other gods, and his heart was divided. He lost his focus, forgot his purpose, and discovered the futility of life without purpose. He became a weak, self-indulgent ruler, no longer the strong, godly leader he once was.

When the children of Israel wandered directionless and confused in the wilderness for forty years, the Lord reminded them, *"I bore you on eagles' wings and brought you to Myself"* (Exodus 19:4). God had a specific purpose and destination for His people, as a nation and as individuals. Notice, He didn't just direct His people to a promised land where they would flourish physically. His first priority was to *bring them to Himself.*

The world today is still a wilderness and God is still directing His people—*but the first destination will always be back into fellowship and a close relationship with Him.*

Every time God's people stopped asking Him for direction, they started wandering and got lost. Because He loved them faithfully, as He loves us today, God allowed whatever was necessary to get them back on course. Later the prophet Isaiah wrote, *"Those who wait on the LORD shall renew their strength; they shall mount up with wings like eagles, they shall run and not be weary, they shall walk and not faint"* (Isaiah 40:31).

When God's purpose is fulfilled in your life, your strength will not only be renewed, but your life will begin to soar to new heights.

FULFILLING MY PURPOSE WILL RESTORE MY JOY

One of God's purposes for your life is to be filled with joy. *"These things I have spoken to you,"* Jesus explained, *"that My joy may remain in you, and that your joy may be full"* (John 15:11). Jesus made it clear that joy is definitely part of His plan for our lives.

For the joy set before Him, the Bible says, Jesus endured the Cross (Hebrews 12:2). Jesus fulfilled the passion of His heart—the redemption of the human race. So great was His love, so powerful was His passion, that He laid everything down. He drank of the bitter cup, He gave everything up for the passion that moved Him.

Jesus lived with a specific call on His life. He knew there would be pain. But He also knew that only in fulfilling His purpose would there be true joy.

Jesus didn't try to do everything. He didn't heal every person He met. He didn't change the government or clean up the environment. He knew His purpose and focused on it.

When we try to meet every need, agree to every committee, attend every seminar or church service, we get overwhelmed with obligations and lose our effectiveness—and our joy.

That was the beauty of the disciples' lives as they followed Jesus. They had a mission. They had purpose. They didn't worry about accomplishing it; they just focused on following Jesus, step by step, village to village, city to city, wherever He went. And they were filled with joy.

PURPOSE REVEALED

The most essential step in discovering your life's purpose is what Jesus told Martha. He elaborated later to His disciples, *"I am the vine, you are the branches. He who abides in Me, and I in him, bears much fruit; for without Me you can do nothing"* (John 15:5).

I often read these words out loud, highlight them, underline them—whatever it takes to remind myself: *My purpose in life is revealed as I abide in Him.*

Solomon needed to discover this principle. The apostle Paul knew it. One of the greatest revelations of his life and ministry was, *"I can do all things through Christ who strengthens me"* (Philippians 4:13). The opposite of that is, without Christ, we can do nothing of lasting and real value.

Our Christian life is not about what we humans can do for God. We put so much pressure on ourselves to perform and to do. Our purpose is revealed as we realize *what He has done for us.*

God's will is manifested in two ways: The *perfect will* of God, and the *permissive will* of God.

If you could push a magic button to see what God has in store for you if you follow His perfect will ... and if you would give yourself to it ... you would be so blown away and so inspired that you wouldn't be able to humble yourself fast enough as you realize the great and wonderful things God wants to do for you.

Then there's His permissive will. God gave us a marvelous attribute called free will. He allows us to choose *not* to follow His perfect plan. He permits us to take matters into our own hands. But let me tell you a secret, learned after twenty some years of counseling disillusioned people. *Life's disappointments are always the result of following our own understanding.* Rather than follow God's path, we take our own—and then wonder why life didn't turn out quite the way we thought it should.

There is hope, however, even when we stray from God's perfect will. The Bible promises us that *"all things work together for good for those who love God, to those who are the called according to His purpose"* (Romans 8:28).

Most of us, if we're honest, really think, *well, most things turn out for good. Somehow we'll muddle through.* But Paul wrote that ALL things work together for good, not just some things!

God uses every experience in our lives to teach us of our need for Him. A friend of mine remembered sitting in the basement of an old church in Los Angeles when he was seven years old, and earnestly raising his hand to accept Jesus into his life. Nothing in his short life up to that moment gave him any understanding of what this decision was all about. For years, he had no idea what really happened. He eventually shrugged it off as one of those childhood things.

Years later, in a moment of great need, he cried out to God and everything he had heard in that basement rushed to the forefront of his memory—the love of God, Jesus' declaration that He would never leave him nor forsake him. My friend recalled feeling as if his whole life hinged on the spiritual transaction he made with God as a young boy. He understood that God loved him and would indeed work all things for good in his life.

God's Word never comes back void; every time His Word impacts your life—whether through worship, church, someone talking to you, or in prayer—it's always used by Him for good in your life. Look at exactly what He says and hang on to this promise: *"So is my word that goes out from my mouth: it will not return to me empty, but will accomplish what I desire and achieve the purpose for which I sent it. You will go out in joy and be led forth in peace ... "* (Isaiah 55:11–12 NIV).

Even through our painful experiences—*especially* our pain—God shapes our personalities and our characters. He never wastes a hurt! Out of the wounds you have suffered, out of your tragedies, failures, and mistakes, and out of your heartaches and fears will emerge a passion and purpose that will direct and shape your life.

Knowing that all of our experiences are under God's provision is comforting. He takes us places where He wants us to be to provide the external circumstances that will mold and shape our lives.

MARCH TO A MISSION

My friend Ron Jenson proposes that each of us needs to "march to a mission." By this he means, "living with a sense of destiny, of passion and excitement and meaning. It means knowing that you are living your life in a significant way."[29] A sense of mission gives meaning and purpose to life. Part of our purpose, then, is to have a mission. What's the difference?

Simply put, I believe it's this:

Our purpose in life is to know God. Our mission in life is to reveal God.

If you are a believer, then you have a specific function in the body of Christ. There's something about you that no other human being can duplicate, an affect you have on people's lives that no one else can have. That's your gift, the Creator's *call* upon your life.

Another word for *call* is vocation. Vocation is our life's work, how we occupy our time on this earth. Martin Luther called vocation a "mask" for God. Behind every occupation and role in life hides the heart of God. Beneath the grease and grime of an auto mechanic, the love of Christ works. Behind the white coat of a doctor, the love of God heals and comforts. A mother who scrubs her way through housework and diapers glorifies God through her service to her family. Martin Luther is often quoted, "A dairy maid can milk cows to the glory of God."

God does not need our works, but He longs to bless those who are needy through us. You can be a gift from God to the world when you allow Him to reveal Himself through you, like love poured out through a flawed, but very beloved vessel.

Solomon's greatest achievement was not building the temple. Solomon's greatest accomplishments were *made possible* by his greatest moments: his encounters with God, when he knew His love, and experienced His indescribable glory.

Chapter Seven
KING OF THE WORLD!

THE WARNING

*W*HILE *Jerusalem slept, their king paced. He climbed the steps up to the high point of the temple. They led him to the pinnacle on the eastside, where he stood in the quiet night, taking in every distant shadow, hill, or building silhouette that landscaped his vast kingdom. Canopied by a clear night and lit by stars and a full moon, the city below him lay quiet, as the day before creation.*

He waited for dawn to bring alive the dormant communities. A small light here and there outlined points of the ever-expanding city; the points grew further apart every week as the kingdom stretched far beyond the early boundaries of David. In a few short hours, the dust would stir as the clanking of tools, the workmen's voices, the braying of pack animals, and the cheers of encouragement from passing citizens would herald the greatest building boom in the nation's history.

His kingdom was twice as large David's. Beyond the last

hill he could barely see the staidly shadows of the main fortress cities—Hazor, Megiddo, and Gezer. Israel stood protected from all directions. The store cities overflowed with stockpiled food and supplies, while in the open lands his stables housed horses and chariots, groomed and waiting for his command.

Tributes poured in from within and without his kingdom. Into the port of Eilat, by the Red Sea, his massive navy of ships cargoed in a continuous flow of silver, gold, ivory, spices, animals, and precious stones—gifts sent by kings and queens from every known part of the world, eager to stay in his favor. Mingled with their awe for his accomplishments was a satisfying dose of fear. His craftsmen worked the precious materials into shields and harnesses, cups and jewelry and furniture … everything in the kingdom glistened with beauty and wealth, reflecting the prestige and honor the world lavished upon him.

From his vantage point, he watched the city wake up. First, in the dark before dawn, the servants began morning preparations. Fires were lit, walkways swept, and the clatter of food preparation broke the stillness, as if a painted canvas had come to life. He smiled at the sight of slaves, many born in his own household, serving his people, who had once themselves been a nation of slaves. The hardest labor, the crushing work that once oppressed his people, now fell on the backs of conquered Canaanites and other foreigners. Solomon gloated at the irony. Vineyards, fountains, gardens, pools, and elegant living quarters sprang from their toil. Their suffering now provided his luxury.

He anticipated the new day—his customary visit to Etham, with its beautiful gardens watered by rivulets of clear water, would be made all the more pleasant by his most recent gifts of horses and chariots from neighboring kings. These increased his fleet of chariots to fourteen hundred and his horses to over twenty-two thousand.

He pictured them; his chariots would be polished, gleaming in the sun. His horses, exercised and groomed to incomparable beauty and swiftness, would be ridden by the tallest, strongest, most handsome young men in the kingdom—twelve thousand strong. The young men would be clothed in the richest purple and fitted with the finest armor, bows, and arrows. Their long, flowing hair was sprinkled daily with real gold flecks, creating an aura of brilliance and light—while he, Solomon, David's son, rode in his chariot above them all, down the rich blackstone causeway, clothed in a white robe and surrounded by adoration.

Every day, returning to Jerusalem, he gazed in awe at the city set on the hill. Every day the beauty of the temple, covered in plates of gold and reflecting the first rising of the sun with a fiery splendor, astonished him. The parts that weren't gold were polished white, causing the temple to appear from a distance as a mountain covered with snow.

The image of it all thrilled his imagination as he waited for sunrise.

"Solomon."

The voice surprised him. He turned.

"I have heard your prayer."

Solomon remembered praying. Such a short time ago, yet so much had transpired. He remained quiet, waiting. The last time the Lord spoke to him in the night, He offered him a great gift.

"If you follow Me as your father David did, then I will see to it that you and your descendants will always be kings of Israel; but if you don't follow Me, if you refuse the laws I have given you, and worship idols, then I will destroy My people from this land."

The first light began to erase away the darkness. The temple shadows sharpened as day broke. Solomon pondered the warning a moment. He shook off a cold shudder and told himself to be careful ... be wise. He didn't want to think about what might be wrong, as he turned to greet the day.

His kingdom came alive below him as sunlight painted brilliant colors across the landscape. As far as he could see, he ruled. No end in sight, no limit to what lay ahead—he had eclipsed the shadow of his father David. His wealth and power exceeded any king that had ever reigned over Jerusalem. He, Solomon, reigned as king of the world.[30]

§

DOWN IN THE DOLDRUMS

Success may flatter us on the outside as significance eludes us from the inside.

—Os Guinness

A boat drifted on the quiet sea. Hours ago, a storm raged, tossing the fragile vessel about like a toy; the captain and crew held onto life tenaciously as they steered through the storm and prayed for providence to give them a respite.

Days before, the winds had been their friends, powering them across acres of water, their cargo full of profits and their anticipation of success as palatable as the salty air.

But now, they drifted. Their cargo was deposited, money now fattened their pockets, and the storm had been weathered—all was calm. The sun shimmered brightly on the flat expanse of water. No danger lurked. No mountains of water threatened to swallow them. No winds battered their tired ship. Nothing. They had reached the doldrums, the calm near the equator where nothing threatens and after a while nothing excites—a place no sailor enjoys for very long.

Isn't life like that? When we are motivated by a goal or a need to survive, we work long hours, toiling to achieve, to get to the finish line, to meet the deadline, or to reach a certain level of income. When we get there, it's a relief to sit back, relax, and enjoy the fruits of our labor. It's nice to cruise for a while. But if we keep cruising, but go nowhere, stagnation sets in. A deadly boredom fills the vacuum. Spiritual dullness numbs our souls and sets us up for a dangerous fall.

Remember David and Bathsheba? The Bible tells us that David's sin of adultery and murder took place, "In the spring, at the time when kings go off to war, and David sent Joab out ..." (see 2 Samuel 11:1). David stayed home and relaxed while his men were at war. David fell while under the spell of the doldrums.

Now we come to a part of Solomon's life where he's cruising. As he stood on that pinnacle, surveying his domain, do you think he felt satisfied? Content? I think so. After all, hadn't he just completed what God had asked of him? And wasn't his success due almost entirely to the wisdom the Lord had given him? So why the warning? Was God trying to spoil Solomon's day? Couldn't He have just let Solomon enjoy this moment of glory and save the admonitions for later? Or did the Lord know something about human nature? Solomon, for all his wisdom, was as vulnerable as his father before him.

Is God issuing the same warning to us?

"But wait," you say. "I'm not Solomon. I'll never be that rich or successful. When will I be able to cruise? Why would such a warning ever apply to my little life?"

A friend of mine from Missouri often speaks with fondness about the rural life in which she grew up. Her hardworking grandparents were comfortably well-off, but she admits that her relatively modest suburban home in Southern California would probably have looked like a palace to her grandmother, had she lived to see it.

We think of Solomon as unspeakably wealthy—beyond our comprehension. But, even with our bills, taxes, and financial pressures, if we were to take an inventory of our material goods, relative to Solomon's day, we might be amazed.

We are wealthy in ways we can't appreciate. We have cars, televisions, microwaves, wall-to-wall carpeting, running water, electricity, abundant food supplies, access to money and spending power through ATMs and credit cards—things that would make Solomon envious! Heating and air conditioning in our homes and cars allow us to control our climate. Technology and medical advances make our physical lives comfortable in ways Solomon could not have imagined. We take them for granted because they have become the norm for our culture. We live in an abundantly affluent and comfort-driven society.

We can all stand on our own individual pinnacles and survey what we own and what we have accomplished—and remain as oblivious as Solomon to the warning of the Lord.

Let's look at what God actually said to Solomon at that moment:

> So Solomon finished building the Temple as well as his own palace. He completed what he had planned to do.

One night the Lord appeared to Solomon and told him, "I have heard your prayer and have chosen this Temple as the place where I want you to sacrifice to me. If I shut up the heavens so that there is no rain, or if I command the locust swarms to eat up all of your crops, or if I send an epidemic among you, then if my people will humble themselves and pray, and search for me, and turn from their wicked ways, I will hear them from heaven and forgive their sins and heal their land. I will listen, wide awake, to every prayer made in this place. For I have chosen this Temple and sanctified it to be my home forever; my eyes and my heart shall always be here.

"As for yourself, if you follow me as your father David did, then I will see to it that you and your descendants will always be the kings of Israel; but if you don't follow me, if you refuse the laws I have given you and worship idols, then I will destroy my people from this land of mine that I have given them, and this Temple shall be destroyed even though I have sanctified it for myself. Instead, I will make it a public horror and disgrace. Instead of its being famous, all who pass by will be incredulous.

" 'Why has the Lord done such a terrible thing to this land and to this Temple?' they will ask.

"And the answer will be, 'Because his people abandoned the Lord God of their fathers, the God who brought them out of the land of Egypt, and they worshiped other gods instead. That is why he has done all this to them.' "

—2 Chronicles 7:11–22 TLB

God didn't issue a light slap on the wrist or a gentle, "Be careful, now!" Bells, whistles, and flashing red lights were going off and Solomon ignored them. How?

What was Solomon's great sin? History tells us that he indeed went down the slippery slope of idolatry and disobedience. But where did it start? He answered that question with his own words: *"My son, do not forget my law, but let your heart keep my commands"* (Proverbs 3:1).

Solomon's heart had turned, slowly. The hardness and coldness toward God crept over his once healthy soul like a cruel disease that silently invades a healthy body, unnoticed, until it's too late.

Dr. Paul Brand was one of the world's leading experts on the treatment of Hansen's disease, more commonly known as leprosy. One day, while working as a missionary in India, he watched horrified as a person reached into a fire to retrieve a potato that had fallen in the flame. In another instance, when Dr. Brand struggled to open a latch, a ten-year-old boy said to him, "Oh, sahib doctor, let me try," and wrenched open the latch. When Dr. Brand saw drops of blood splatter to the ground, he realized that the boy had ripped his flesh to the bone without feeling a thing. Another man, intending to wash his face, blinded himself with scalding water.

Leprosy is cruel, Dr. Brand explained, in a way no other disease is cruel. It acts like an anesthetic, numbing the nerve cells of hands, feet, nose, ears, and eyes. That might not sound so bad at first; most diseases are feared for the pain they induce. But the terror of this "painless" disease is the damage wreaked upon a numbed and unmindful victim, who "forgets" to defend himself against destructive situations.[31]

Men like Solomon don't just decide one day to turn their backs on the Lord and walk away from His blessings. It is a slow, sneaky process—like leprosy.

NOONDAY DEMONS

Did you know that during the reign of both David and Solomon, Israel possessed only about ten percent of what God had promised them? Not even David, the sweet Psalmist of Israel, the "man after God's own heart," or Solomon, who elevated the children of Abraham to the status of superpower, experienced all that God had for them. Knowing what God did with just ten percent, we can only wonder what might have been if Solomon had received it all! The wealthiest, wisest, most powerful man on the face of the earth settled for a mere portion of what God intended for him and his nation.

How many of us are living with the same small portion of God's blessings? Over seven thousand promises in the Bible give us the hope of abundant life. How many of those promises have you appropriated? I ask myself the same question every day. Truly, there is a little of Solomon in each of us.

Peter Marshall used to say, "Today's Christians are like deep-sea divers encased in suits designed for many fathoms deep, bravely marching forth to pull plugs out of bathtubs."[32]

What holds us back? Os Guinness suggests that *sloth*—classically known as the fourth deadly sin—is the culprit. Laziness and general "slobbiness" come to mind when I think of the word *sloth*. But Guinness defines it as "a condition of explicitly spiritual dejection that has given up on the pursuit of God, the true, the good, and the beautiful. Sloth is inner despair ... that finally slumps into an attitude of 'Who cares?' ... It is a sluggishness of spirit, feeling, and mind that eventually overcomes the body like an after-lunch languor." Medieval thinkers called it the "noonday demon."[33]

Call it the doldrums, spiritual leprosy, slothfulness, or demons—this state of spiritual apathy eventually leads to boredom, discontent, hedonism, and a constant need for gratification. A subtle spiritual malady hardens our hearts, causing us to turn from the Giver to the gifts; to glory in what we have, to want more, to never be satisfied, to love and desire things for their own sake, apart from God. Slowly, we are changed inside, and become less and less our true selves as we turn into caricatures of who God created and gifted us to be. Slowly, we slip from reality into unreality, anesthetizing the deepest part of our souls. Day by day, moment by moment, choice by choice, in thousands of little ways, our passion for the Lord and our passion for the life He desires for us are dulled, much like the numbing effects of leprosy.

Søren Kierkegaard, decrying the spiritual sloth of his era, wrote, "Let others complain that the times are wicked. I complain that they are paltry; for they are without passion. Their lusts are staid and sluggish, their passions sleepy."

No wonder Jesus said about lukewarm believers, "I will spit you out of My mouth" (see Revelation 3:16). He wants no part of slothful spirituality, because He knows it will eventually destroy us. God's exhortations to Solomon—*"humble yourself ... pray ... seek My face ... follow Me"*—were based purely on what He knows to be best for His people.

The Lord saw Solomon slipping into the comfort zone, where it is easy to shift into neutral and never do anything meaningful again. That's when our spirits shrivel up, our vision dies, and along with it, our hopes, dreams, and faith. The tragedy is that when we choose not to pursue the other ninety percent of God's blessings, we eventually lose the ten percent we already possess.

God was reaching out to pull Solomon back into the blessing zone.

FIVE STEPS TOWARD BACKSLIDING

Solomon followed a classic pattern toward degeneration. Five easy steps, demonstrated for us centuries later by the apostle Peter.

What did the richest, wisest king in the world and an impetuous, poorly educated fisherman have in common? More than you might imagine. One day, they each found themselves on top of their own little worlds, and the next, falling into a place they never thought they'd go.

STEP ONE: PUFFED UP WITH PRIDE

Just as Solomon could stand at the top of an impressive building surveying the domain he had built and ruled, so a rough fisherman from the shores of Galilee found himself in the heady position of leading a revolution that would build an even greater kingdom—an eternal one, ruled by the Messiah, the Son of the living God.

One night, Jesus gathered His disciples around Him and shared His last supper with them. Gently, He warned them, *"All of you will be made to stumble because of Me this night, for it is written, 'I will strike the Shepherd, and the sheep of the flock will be scattered.' But after I have been raised, I will go before you to Galilee"* (Matthew 26:31).

Before His crucifixion, Jesus wanted His disciples to know that He understood what would happen. *Look,* He was saying, *I know what you will do, but I will still love you and forgive you, and I'll be waiting for you the morning of the resurrection.*

But Peter couldn't accept that.

Peter loved the Lord with a passion, but by now, he had become enamored with his position as one of Jesus' right-hand guys. After all, just days before this somber dinner, he had said something pretty amazing, and well, downright brilliant.

He still warmed with satisfaction at the memory. They had all just arrived at Caesarea Philippi. Numerous stories circulated ahead of them about how they fed five thousand people with a few loaves and fishes. And he, Peter, had amazed everyone—especially himself—by actually walking on water with the Master. The sick were healed, demons were driven away, and Jesus stood up to the Pharisees and confounded them with His wisdom. They were amazing days.

Then, arriving at Philippi in the wake of all these miracles, Jesus stopped to ask His disciples, "Who do men say that I am?" Simon Peter had never felt surer about anything in his life. While the others quoted popular opinion—"John the Baptist," "Elijah!"—Peter spoke the words that had been forming in his mind and heart like a dim light growing brighter and brighter until it finally burst forth as a revelation: "You are the Messiah, the Son of the living God!" (see Matthew 16:13,16).

It was true! He knew in that moment that he spoke *truth*, emanating from heaven, revealed in his heart, pronounced by his own lips. Indeed, Jesus confirmed it by answering, *"Blessed are you, Simon Bar-Jonah, for flesh and blood has not revealed this to you, but My Father who is in heaven"* (Matthew 16:17). Jesus told Peter He would give him the "keys to the kingdom" and that he would prevail against hell and build a church. After all that, how could Jesus imagine that Peter would stumble?

"No, Lord!" Peter blurted out. "Even if everyone else deserts You, I won't."

Jesus looked at Peter and said, "The truth is, this very night, before the cock crows at dawn, you will deny Me three times" (see Matthew 26:34).

"I'd rather die first!" Peter responded. He was so sure of himself—and so ready to ignore God's warning. After all, he had the keys to the kingdom!

Peter did indeed deny his Lord three times that night. "I will never stumble; I will never fail" are words that no human being can afford to utter. From Solomon to Peter, to each of us, we need to realize that we are vulnerable to the greatest of all temptations: Pride. Is this fair? Are we humans just so prone to ultimate failure that we can't even enjoy success for a time and feel secure in it? Does anyone *successfully* succeed?

I don't have the answer to that, except to listen to the warnings of the Lord. Solomon ignored them, Peter denied them, and both ended up with regrets they lived with until the day they died. But I do know that no one backslides overnight. Specific increments of behavior and attitude lead us down that path. Perhaps if we recognize these steps, we can stop before we go too far.

STEP TWO: PRAYERLESSNESS

Soon after Peter's passionate declaration of loyalty, Jesus and the disciples arrived at Gethsemane. Jesus asked the others to sit outside the garden area while He went to pray, but He took Peter, James, and John, His closest friends, with Him.

Jesus longed for companionship that night. He faced a terrifying ordeal and wanted to prepare Himself. He asked His closest friends to pray with Him, but after a brief time, found them asleep.

"What! Could you not watch with Me one hour?" He asked (Matthew 26:40).

Even Peter, with all his zeal, could not make prayer a priority. The pattern is typical. We get a little cocky, a little too sure of ourselves and our accomplishments, and pretty soon prayer doesn't seem all that necessary. After all, we get pretty tired from all that accomplishing and need our rest and relaxation.

Solomon did the same thing. He began to take more pleasure in his gifts than in the Giver. He got so busy building and acquiring that he forgot how he had once prayed to the Lord with such passion: *"LORD God of Israel, there is no God in heaven or on earth like You, who keep Your covenant and mercy with Your servants who walk before You with all their hearts"* (2 Chronicles 6:14).

When prayer slips out of your life, it means you have more confidence in yourself than in the Lord, and that you have quit walking with Him with all your heart. This always leads to the next step.

Step Three: Taking Matters into Your Own Hands

Once we stop praying, we're forced to rely upon our own resources to deal with life. Peter was a great one for that. When he finally woke up at Gethsemane, after Jesus had finished praying, it was to face Judas Iscariot and all the soldiers who had come to take Jesus to Calvary. Impetuous Peter, perhaps still sleepy, but certainly not inspired by prayer, quickly took matters into his own hands. He grabbed a sword and brashly sliced off the ear of the servant of the high priest—which solved nothing and made the situation more dangerous.

Jesus quickly told Peter to put his sword away: *"Do you think I cannot now pray to My Father, and He will provide Me with more than twelve legions of angels?"* (Matthew 26:53). Jesus had spent enough time praying through the night to know His Father's will. There was no need to try to change the course of events with impetuous heroics. Jesus then reached out and healed the damaged ear, performing the last recorded miracle of His earthly ministry.

Even then, Jesus took the time to "fix" one of Peter's blunders. How many miracles has He performed in our lives to cover our fumbles and mistakes? I don't think we'll ever know until we get to heaven.

The "God helps those who help themselves" platitude that gets thrown around as if it were Scripture (it's not) is one of the great deceptions of our day. God helps those who *can't* help themselves, and those who call upon His name. His *grace* is sufficient. We are not sufficient in ourselves.

Solomon realized this when he humbly prayed in the beginning of his reign, asking for wisdom and guidance to build the temple and to lead the kingdom. But once it was all done, we don't see much evidence of him turning to the Lord or to godly counsel. He began to negotiate with the world on his own, as we shall soon see.

STEP FOUR: FOLLOWING FROM AFAR

Peter just keeps digging himself in deeper and deeper. After Gethsemane, he had a chance to correct his course. But the accumulation of pride, prayerlessness, and self-sufficiency had put such a gap between him and the Lord that now, even in Jesus' darkest hour, brave, brash "I will never stumble" Peter began to follow Jesus from afar (Matthew 26:58).

Peter stumbled toward the crucifixion, too cowardly to walk alongside his friend, too weak to trust in God's plans. He couldn't leave, out of guilt, but he couldn't help, and he couldn't encourage the others. All the leadership abilities he had so zealously coveted withered under his fear and guilt. The last step toward backsliding became almost inevitable.

STEP FIVE: WARMED BY THE ENEMY'S FIRE

Peter followed the soldiers as they headed toward the high priest's house, where they were taking Jesus. He kept Jesus in sight, but from a distance. Perhaps shivering from the chill before dawn or from the fear and confusion rising inside him, he was drawn toward a fire kindled in the courtyard, and sat down to warm himself. Did he realize that these were the very people conspiring against the Lord? Did he stop to think that he was warming himself by the enemy's fire? He was apparently so caught up in his own misery that he had lost all discernment.

When a servant girl looked intently at him and declared, *"This man was also with Him,"* brave, heroic Peter denied knowing the Lord—just as Jesus had predicted—three times before the rooster crowed and the day broke (Luke 22:56).

The Scripture tells us that Peter wept bitterly over his betrayal. He had ignored all the warnings and continued to blindly bumble through each step on his way down.

But the story of Peter doesn't end there. Jesus was true to His Word. He met the disciples after the resurrection. He particularly sought out Peter, ministered to him, forgave him, and reaffirmed Peter's calling to build the church and feed God's sheep (John, chapter 21). Peter found sweet forgiveness and restoration.

Peter found what is available to anyone who ventures down the road that leads to a backslidden state: forgiveness and restoration, if only we are willing to receive them. God's love surrounds us in a thousand ways, yet we limit that love by what we are willing to receive. We keep thinking that God is interested in what we have to offer Him, when in fact it is God who is rich and is looking for willing recipients for all the wealth of His gifts of love.

But what about our friend Solomon? He once turned to the Lord, and received His blessings. But like Peter, he ignored the warnings. If Peter warmed himself by the enemy's fire, Solomon stepped right in—like a leper whose senses are so numbed he thinks the fires can't burn him—and fanned the flames.

Part Three
REDEMPTION

Redemption is the liberation of man.

—John Mackay

Chapter Eight

THE QUEEN OF SHEBA AND OTHER FOREIGN WOMEN

"O king, do not look upon me for I am black ... though lovely. Like the tents of Kedar ..."

Solomon set down his wine goblet and looked at the queen. Was she mocking him? Quoting his own poetry back to him, she unsettled him ... again.

The significance of Kedar was not lost on him. The name meant powerful and dark—and she was both.

"Makeda," he said, using her personal name. He was about to continue the poetic bantering, when she interrupted him. She realized he was trying to seduce her and smiled kindly, reaching out to touch his hand.

"Everything I heard about you in my own country is true!" She studied his face intently, as if to move him beyond the carnal games. "I did not believe what they said until I came and saw with my own eyes. Your wisdom is far greater than I

could ever have imagined. How happy your men must be! How happy these servants who stand before you continually. I am overwhelmed!"

He was gratified. It had been many years since he had tried so hard to impress a woman. Her beauty distracted him, but when she challenged him with questions and sat enthralled at his wisdom, he felt happier than he had in years. They talked for hours, often into the night. She listened to him with a look of joyous rapture, almost like a woman in love, receiving a precious gift from her beloved. Like a melody that triggers a memory, their exchanges reminded him of a time long ago. He wanted to keep her.

Since the hour she had arrived, the queen had unsettled Solomon's court. She would never be another wife acquired for political gain, or a mere concubine—or a shepherd girl. Even her arrival had been a staggering sight.

For days, his servants had kept him updated about the vast spectacle on the horizon. A field of soldiers, servants, and animals shimmered in the distance, like wheat waving in a soft breeze. Two young shepherds saw them first and ran to spread news of the exotic sight. The queen and her entourage escorted over seven hundred camels laden with gold, sweet spices, and precious stones—magnificent even to Solomon's lavish court.

A special apartment had been prepared for her lodging; servants laid out the best food and at least eleven changes of garments daily. Responding to her desire for knowledge, Solomon seated her on a throne, next to his, so she could observe his daily judgments. He spared nothing, and she delighted in it all. She praised him with words, looked at him with admiration, *and finally presented him with one hundred twenty talents of gold and an abundance of rare spices and stones such as Israel had never seen before.*

Not for years had a woman fascinated him as she had. He wanted to woo her into his court, to declare his love—and she was using his own poetry to deflect him.

Six months had fled by, and now she informed him that she needed to return to her land. When he tried to protest, she quieted him with more praise. "Blessed be the Lord your God, who delighted in you," she said. "He chose you and set you on the throne of Israel. How the Lord must love Israel—for He gave you to them as their king!"

But Solomon wasn't thinking of the Lord as she spoke. He watched her, entranced by her dark, intelligent eyes, and wondered how he could keep her —at least for one more night.

He had staged a final, grand feast to say farewell —and to try to convince her to stay—which lasted late into the night. And then, she left as she had arrived, surrounded by a sea of wealth and a city of attendants. As her entourage rode away, the king felt the last remnants of his heart slipping away with her. Love, long buried in the past, would remain buried. Nothing remained but to escape into indulgence. So be it.

From that day on, every dark and beautiful woman, every foreign and exotic eye that offered herself to him, he took ... and took. He took from the Moabites, the Ammonites, the Edomites, the Sidonians, and the Hittites until he lost count, though his advisors informed him that he possessed over one thousand wives and concubines. And with every woman, a new graven image entered the temple.

Every hopeful bloom of new love inevitably ended in nothing more than a new addition to his harem. He felt obliged to allow the women, those who had given themselves to him, to have their gods—they would certainly never have his heart. Besides, he found these strange religions intellectually stimulating. He sought after Ashtoreth and built altars to Chemosh and Molech. He brought their images into the temple, and allowed his wives to burn their incense and sacrifice their offerings, filling the air with a thick, ungodly stench.

The priests looked upon him with guarded disdain, and silently cheered the brave prophet who dared to speak: "The Lord is angry with you, because your heart has turned."

But Solomon no longer heard the voice of the Lord. His mind and heart were cluttered by the din of new spirits vying for his soul, drowning out the psalms of his father, and silencing the poetic songs that had once echoed in his heart. Even the Queen of Sheba, who had awakened for a moment his passion and his wisdom, began to seem like a half-remembered dream. All of it had become a stilled song he could no longer hear, one that no longer rang in harmony with his life.

He stood one evening at his familiar perch, looking down on his kingdom, as he had done for years. He watched the bustle of the day slowing down, the long shadows drawing themselves over the city's life. Fear struck him as he recognized how dark it was growing, how dim the temple looked, with no sun to reflect off its alabaster walls. Darkness seemed to be slowing him down as well.

He noticed his wrinkling hands and knew that his lusts couldn't stop time. His pleasures could no longer disguise his weakened forces. "The eye is not satisfied with seeing, nor the ear filled with hearing," he recited, words he had written but only now acknowledged. He looked up into the heavens and heard nothing, and suddenly missed who he had once been. "It's all vanity!" he cried. "There's nothing new. Nothing more to do. It all means nothing. It's all in vain. All of it. Vain foolishness." He wept bitterly, as the sorrow that swept over his soul seemed unbearable.[34]

———————————— § ————————————

A man who has lost his way is not always a person who is extraordinarily sinful or wanton in his desire to rebel against God. It's not usually the fiery rebel who falls into a spiritual void. Apathy and boredom relieved by carnal pleasures inevitably lead to spiritual dullness.

Whether Solomon succeeded in his quest to seduce the Queen of Sheba, we don't know. Some have speculated that Solomon wrote the *Song of Solomon* for her. Scripture is silent, but history, particularly Ethiopia's, claims that they bore a son, who succeeded his mother in ruling Ethiopia and produced a long line of heirs up to Emperor Haile Selassie (early 1900s).[35]

Most of my research, however, reinforces the shepherd girl scenario; but I have no doubt that Solomon may have used his poetic prowess to impress the Queen of Sheba and the women who followed. It's as if he tried over and over to recreate the love he once knew.

Historically, we don't know what finally happened to the Shulamite girl. The last time we see her in Scripture, she is being brought in to keep David warm and is the object of a deadly rivalry between Solomon and his brother Adonijah. There is speculation that she was brought into Solomon's harem, then forgotten when he became enamored with his power and wealth. It has also been suggested that she returned home, married a shepherd boy, and lived happily ever after. While her fate is unclear, we do know that she represents a time in Solomon's life when love was true and faithful and could be counted on.

But now, Solomon had lost the romance of life. He had allowed his relationship with the Lord to whither; he threw all wisdom to the wind, and lost his passion for everything important. In another more modern day story, a friend of mine experienced the same thing.

PASSION GONE COLD

My friend Jack* woke up every morning depressed. He rose before daylight, pulled on his construction boots and work jeans, then crept quietly downstairs. Leaning against the kitchen counter, he would stare out the window and wait for his coffee to brew. Balancing the steaming mug and the piles of paper shoved under his arm, he left before his family began to wake.

He knew that every morning nowadays his wife pulled the covers up close around her neck as soon as he eased out of bed. She kept her eyes tightly closed as she listened to his morning ritual, and waited to hear the door shut and his truck engine chug to life before she rose. He saw her watch through their bedroom window as he drove away. There was a time when he would never have left without a kiss and a hug. But then, she used to get up with him most mornings and fuss over his clothes or make sure he had a lunch and didn't forget important papers … or a doctor's appointment … or a teacher's conference.

He remembered how they would sit together, drink their coffee, and watch the sunrise. In quiet voices, they discussed the day's plans, the kids, the bills. Sometimes they prayed, sometimes they just started the day together.

_____

* _The names in this story have been changed._

When he knew she had been up at night with a sick child or finishing a project, he would snuggle her into the covers, whisper for her to stay cozy and get some sleep, then be sure to make enough coffee for both of them. He liked her to come downstairs to that welcoming aroma. But all that stopped. Now, he left the coffee pot empty and she never got up.

My friend came in to talk to me one day. He told me how he drove to work every day, watched the sunrise alone, and wondered how things got so messed up. He used to pray while he drove. He used to be thankful for the blessings of work and family. "I used to love my life," he exclaimed. Slamming his fist on the table between us, he spit out bitter words of complaint and anger. "Now all I do is pay bills, argue with Sandy, argue with my kids, go to work every day, and do the same ___ thing over and over."

"But look at your life," I protested. "Look at how blessed you are. I remember when you were struggling to pay rent on a little apartment and literally prayed for your daily meals. The Lord has blessed you with a family and friends who love you. You own your own company, a great house … you are loved and respected at church. What's wrong?"

"What's wrong is that none of it means anything anymore. I feel dead inside."

I wish this story had a happy ending. I wish I could say that as I read Scripture with him, counseled him, and prayed with him and for him, one day he woke up and climbed out of the spiritual bog he had fallen into. I wish a light had gone on in his head and heart and he could have fallen in love with the Lord and with life again. But that didn't happen. Not yet anyway.

He was a man who appeared to be winning at the game of life, but was in reality desperately losing everything—because he had lost what is most important. He had fallen out of love with the Lord, and as a consequence, with life. I once knew him to be a man filled with the Holy Spirit, on fire with a passion for the Lord. God had richly blessed him.

But he threw it all away. He left his family and embarked on a series of miserable affairs. His business deteriorated into bankruptcy, his wife was committed to a mental hospital for a time, and his kids completely rebelled. One of his sons started dealing drugs and the other dropped out of school. I've never seen a family spiral down into such a devastating state of pain and despair. Slowly, the Lord is restoring the wife and her sons, but my friend is still out there somewhere, a bitter, lonely man—one who used to be on top of the world. He had reached a crossroads in his life and took the wrong turn.

Robert Frost captured this great human dilemma with these poignant lines:

> The woods are lovely, dark and deep
> But I have promises to keep,
> And miles to go before I sleep,
> And miles to go before I sleep.[36]

One part of the speaker would like to stop and enjoy the adventure of entering into the dark and lovely woods. There's a little mystery there, a little of the unknown. Something different from daily life. But the other part of him recognizes the larger responsibilities owed to others; promises he made—perhaps wedding vows—that need to be kept.

For believers, the dark woods might be like that other path Solomon was tempted to follow. Remember the vision he had of wisdom as a beautiful lady? (Proverbs 8, chapter four in this book.) She offered him life filled with joy and abundance and all the adventures he could handle. But another woman enticed him into her snare, tempting him to throw all of God's blessings away for something different—something very wrong.

When the blessings from God replace our relationship with Him, then the joy of the blessings is dulled. Nothing seems so great anymore. Life doesn't even seem worth living—not our lives anyway.

Thank heavens God will pursue us, even down those dark, wrong roads.

ENDEAVORS AND EXPERIMENTS

Solomon took a wrong turn.

As much as Solomon had relished the blessings of the Lord, he now relished his sin.

We first met him as a man in love with the Shulamite, then as a wise man in love with the Lord. Now we meet him as a foolish man who apparently forgot most of the things he wrote in the book of *Proverbs.* He is identified in the first chapter of the book of *Ecclesiastes* as the *"Preacher, the son of David, king in Jerusalem."*

One thing we can grant Solomon, even in his era of folly, is that, in the end, he was honest. The full scope of his attempts to find meaning in life apart from God is plainly spelled out in the book of *Ecclesiastes.* Throwing himself into an endless series of endeavors and experiments, he explains how he tried to be happy.

As a brilliant man with enough wealth to try, explore, and research anything his imagination conjured up, Solomon left no avenue of pleasure, entertainment, or intellectual pursuit untried. No one can accuse him of not "going for it" or not trying to "be all that you can be." He fulfilled every self-help, motivational jingle ever dreamt of.

Throughout the book of *Ecclesiastes*, Solomon tells us that he delved into science, the arts, and philosophy, only to realize that with *"much wisdom is much grief, and he who increases in knowledge increases sorrow"* (Ecclesiastes 1:18).

When that didn't feel good, he threw himself into pleasure, acquiring more wives, more concubines, eating and drinking, surrounding himself with more beautiful gardens and bountiful vineyards. *"Whatever my eyes desired,"* he said, *"I did not keep from them. I did not withhold my heart from any pleasure"* (Ecclesiastes 2: 10). But his materialism, fed by his endless wealth, only led to this dismal conclusion: *"I hated life ... for all is vanity and grasping for wind"* (Ecclesiastes 2:17).

What did he turn to next? What people have always turned to when their souls feel empty: *Religion!*

He didn't return to his former relationship with God. He didn't humble himself before the Lord, repent of his sins, or vow to turn the nation back to God. Rather, he became philosophical, humanitarian ... tolerant.

Perhaps the best known passage of *Ecclesiastes* is chapter three, verses 1–8, which begins, *"To everything there is a season, and a time to every purpose under heaven."*

A brilliant piece of philosophy and poetry, simple yet profound, containing undeniable truth. Truly God-inspired. But, we have to read it in the context of Solomon's life.

He was trying very hard to rationalize his actions. After all, if there's a time for everything to happen and it'll happen regardless of our behavior, how can we be responsible for any of our actions?

A few verses later he said, *"He has made everything beautiful in its time. Also He has put eternity in their hearts, except that no one can find out the work that God does from beginning to end. I know that nothing is better for them than to rejoice, and to do good in their lives"* (3:11,12).

"To do good." That's it! Good works should make everything better and life more meaningful—right? Well, yes and no. It's like religion. It's not a bad thing. It's just not necessarily a good thing if the foundation is all wrong. We go back to one of the original premises of this book: Our motivation for becoming artisans at life and for using God-inspired gifts and wisdom must be rooted in a deep, abiding, passionate relationship with the Lord. Or else, as Solomon sadly discovered, *"Vanity of vanities, all is vanity"* (Ecclesiastes 1:2).

In a short story titled "Araby" by James Joyce (from *The Dubliners*), a young boy embarks on a quest to attend the local bazaar and buy a gift for a girl he yearns to impress. When he finally arrives, the booths are closing, the money is being counted, and the hired help is ready to go home. Cold, dark indifference shoved aside the romantic images his mind had conjured up of what the bazaar was supposed to be like. Where was the fun? The romance? In the end, he suffers a shocking revelation: "Gazing up into the darkness I saw myself as a creature driven and derided by vanity; and my eyes burned with anguish and anger."[37]

That's how I see Solomon. The bazaar-like life he had created for himself was threatening to end like all bazaars do, with the lights out, the workers tired of putting on a happy face, and nothing left but coins to count and dirt to sweep away. The rest—the glitter, the promise of romance and fast fun—was all manufactured for a brief moment. No wonder he cried "Vanity!"

Earlier I compared the material wealth of Solomon with our standard of living today. What about the pleasure factor? Solomon admitted that, *"Whatever my eyes desired I did not keep from them. I did not withhold my heart from any pleasure"* (Ecclesiastes 2:10). Are we so different today?

Our pleasure/entertainment-driven society provides endless means of escape. Movies, theater, unlimited restaurants, television with hundreds of channels, the Internet … everything imaginable, and there appears to be no reason to withhold any pleasure desired by our eyes. We could spend twenty-four hours a day living in a fantasy world.

Modern technology has only served to turn the same old sins into more convenient ones. Nothing much has changed about human nature.

THERE'S NOTHING NEW

This startling fact—that ultimately life is a series of cycles that tend to repeat themselves—frightened Solomon. *"Meaningless! Meaningless! Utterly meaningless!"* he lamented. *"Everything is meaningless. What does a man gain from all his labor at which he toils under the sun?"* (Ecclesiastes 1:2–3 NIV).

He was cynical and depressed. *"Generations come and generations go,"* he said, sounding more like Eeyore the pessimistic donkey than a powerful king, *"but the earth remains forever. The sun rises and the sun sets, and hurries back to where it rises. The wind blows to the south and turns to the north; round and round it goes"* (1:4–6 NIV). He even called his precious wisdom just another sad vanity: *"I applied myself to the understanding of wisdom, and also of madness and folly, but I learned that this, too, is a chasing after the wind. For with much wisdom comes much sorrow; the more knowledge, the more grief"* (1:17–18 NIV).

On and on he complained, bored, dissatisfied, and frustrated.

Do you find yourself asking, *Man, what's he got to be so down about? Doesn't he realize that he has it all?*

If you've ever driven a new car off the lot, you'll understand. Remember that new car smell, and the satisfaction of knowing that every time you turn the ignition, this car will surge to power, unlike the one you just traded in that died at every stop sign? I love driving a new car, with the latest gadgets and innovations—for about six months. Then the new models come out and suddenly mine looks a little dated, ordinary ... used. What looked so cool last year looks a little dorky this year and leaves me feeling unsatisfied, and even a little stupid for thinking I had purchased the *ultimate* driving machine.

Solomon realized, to his horror, that the pleasures of life he cherished so much eventually grew old—like him. He saw his existence through jaded eyes and ceased to enjoy the fruit of his labors.

"There is nothing new under the sun," he decided (1:9). No new movies, cars, computers, houses, fashions, vacations, or other pleasures. In some way, shape, or form, it's all been done before, and none of it is fulfilling.

Solomon once tasted the clear, crystal pure waters of heavenly love ... then he settled for the murky waters of temporary joy, and lost his source of beauty, goodness, and truth—treasures the human soul longs to possess.

EAT, DRINK, AND BE MERRY

How did Solomon lose it? How did one who knew so much and had received so much from God end up in despair?

How do strong believers end up bitter, cynical, and despairing of life?

"OK," you might be thinking. "You've got me. I'm jaded. I'm cynical, and I'm beginning to think Solomon was right. It is all vanity and there's not a lot I can do about it. So eat, drink, and be merry ... for tomorrow we really will die."

A friend said that to me one day. He just quit pretending to be spiritually healthy, and confessed to despair.

I appreciated his honesty, and told him what I have had to tell many people: look up! That sounds cliché, but I've learned that there's a spiritual, emotional, mental, and even physical discipline involved. Turning our eyes, our hearts, and our minds upward, toward the Lord, is an act we have to predetermine to do. We need to ask God for the strength to look up in times of distress.

"Despair is a greater sin than all the sins which provoke it," C.S. Lewis said, his point being that while we cannot control the circumstances of our lives, we can choose how we respond. "Oh yeah?" my friend countered. "What if you're so depressed you can't choose?"

What if your despair is so heavy, that you cannot even think of looking up, either mentally or physically? Cling to the Scriptures: *"O LORD, for You have lifted me up ..."* (Psalm 30) ... *"You, O LORD, are the lifter of my head ..."* (see Psalm 3:3). A cry to God, one move toward Him, and He will answer. His answer may be in the form of friends, family, or counselors, but He will do whatever it takes.

Isaiah the prophet lived in a king's palace, served as a king's prophet, and spoke the Word of the Lord to his nation. He had achieved success *and* significance in his life. Yet, he lacked something—something only God recognized and only God could fulfill. Isaiah 6 gives us the account of Isaiah's revelation.

"Woe is me," cried the same prophet who had spent years pointing his finger, exhorting his people, "Woe to you ..." Now, he said, *"My eyes have seen the King, the LORD of hosts"* (Isaiah 6:5). He heard the angels singing, *"Holy, holy, holy,"* and as he humbled himself before God, he received a fresh vision of the Lord, an anointing, and a renewed passion, empowered and refreshed by God's passion for him.

Kings, prophets, construction workers, pastors, businessmen, teachers, mothers, fathers, adults, and children ... we all desperately need that fresh vision.

My life as a pastor began at the young age of 19, when I began pastoring a church of about five hundred people. Later, Mike MacIntosh, pastor of Horizon Christian Fellowship, invited me to join his ministry team, which proved to be four years of growing, learning, and being part of a dynamic, exciting church.

When the Lord uprooted me, I was confused. I had no idea what to do or where to go. Suddenly, all the exciting and fruitful ministry I had enjoyed came to a screeching halt. I felt scared and hardly practiced what I had preached so often about trusting in the Lord's sovereignty, holiness, and compassion. I had a family to support and felt like a has-been at the age of 25.

I resorted to frustrated bouts with the backyard weeds. Angry and anxious, I picked and pulled and dug, venting my frustration with each weed I yanked and each complaint I muttered. Finally, I decided it was time to have a conversation with the Lord, but all I could say was, "God, I give up. I can barely pray anymore. I'll just stay here and pull weeds. You know where to find me."

Suddenly, the peace of God touched my soul. It wasn't the pastor in me telling myself, *you need to trust God and experience His peace.* I couldn't. I was a wreck. The Lord had heard my cries. He did for me what I couldn't do for myself.

When I calmed down, I heard a small, still voice speak to me about starting a Bible study in the immediate area. The Lord encouraged me to step forward, to follow Him, and He would take care of the details.

That's how the Lord started Maranatha Chapel, the church I am privileged to pastor. I have never forgotten how the Lord took a frustrated, angry, and cynical young man, and showed me Himself, high and lifted up. He revived my faith and filled me with joy—not because of the church or the blessings He has poured upon us, but because of who He is, and what He has chosen to accomplish. I will never forget how He ministered to me, to rid me of vainglory and selfish ambition (a continuing process); nor will I forget His sovereignty, as He proved that He had everything under control. Nor will I forget His compassion, as He reached out to me, poured His peace into my heart, granted me grace, and set my life on course.

I will also say, that was not the only time I've had that experience. As we mature in the Lord, He takes us through deeper and deeper experiences, taking life's hardships and trials and using them to draw us closer to His heart. More than once I have cried with Isaiah, *"Woe is me, for I am undone,"* only to have the Lord once again lift my head and allow me to see Him in all His glory, on the throne, still pursuing me, and still loving me.

We've covered a lot of ground in this chapter, but before we move on, I want to go back to the Queen of Sheba. She represents a pivotal point in Solomon's life. After her, everything changed. Even Jesus commented centuries later, in Matthew 12:42: *"The queen of the South will rise up in the judgment with this generation and condemn it, for she came from the ends of the earth to hear the wisdom of Solomon; and indeed a greater than Solomon is here."*

The Queen of Sheba hungered for wisdom, and I think she may have recognized a heart yearning to love again in Solomon. But she took her entourage and left, leaving the king to his own devices. Did he miss an opportunity for true love again? Legends speculate, history ponders, but what we do know is that God had more to do in Solomon's life. The hardest, and the best, was yet to come.

Chapter Nine
A NIGHT OF PASSION

"*Woe to you, O land, when your king is a child.*"

Solomon wrote the words in a fury. What a fool he had been. A child. He had tried to tell everyone, even the Lord. "I am only a child," he cried one night. God responded with a gift.

Wisdom. He threw down his pen and paced. What does wisdom bring anyway, but more grief? More knowledge brings more sorrow. "What can a man do who succeeds the king?" he cried to himself.

I am the man who succeeded the king, he thought. David, the man after God's heart. Who for all his weaknesses and sin, clung to the grace of God and died a hero, a legend, a triumph. Hard footsteps to follow.

"What did I gain by possessing all this wisdom?" Solomon thought. "The wise man has eyes in his head, while the fool walks in darkness, but the same fate overtakes them both. Even my wisdom was vanity. The wise man, like the fool, will soon be forgotten. How does a wise man die? Just like the fool dies!" he concluded, picking up his pen again.

Solomon sat down, trying to write, trying to forget the

worrisome turmoil brewing outside the palace. He scribbled something quickly, then scratched it out. Where was the poetry that once flowed? The wisdom he longed to put to paper eluded him. His mind felt pressured at the trouble he knew plagued his kingdom. Everything still glittered like white and gold during the day, but a shadow had been cast over the bright scene. The hearts of the people were restless, confused. The slavery he enforced fueled his enemies' resentment. His priests reproached him. Adversaries were springing up all around him.

Hadad the Edomite buzzed about the fringes of the kingdom like an annoying insect, striking in Edom and Syria, wherever he could make trouble. When Solomon was young, David's army raided Edom and killed all the males. Hadad escaped to Egypt and married into Pharaoh's court. Once he learned that David was dead, he began to plan his revenge, waiting for years to strike. Now, with Solomon's kingdom weakening, Hadad was happy to spoil the peace.

Pushing Hadad and the others out of his mind, Solomon tried to reassure himself with thoughts of the still thriving city outside his palace. But the shining images no longer conjured up pride, or joy—instead a sick loathing churned in his stomach. "All my toil, all my plans, all my dreams! Some fool who comes after me will destroy everything. It's all meaningless," he muttered. "I hate my life. All the hard work, the labor under the sun, is grievous. All of it is meaningless, like chasing after the wind."

He sat down to write again, furiously. "Dead flies putrefy the perfumer's ointment and cause it to give off a foul odor. So does a little folly to one respected for wisdom and honor." Has *my folly really been so bad? he wondered, as his pen scratched out the only sound in the room.*

"Your wicked actions have not been concealed from God."

Startled, Solomon turned at the harsh voice. Ahijah, the prophet from Shiloh, stood in the doorway, his arm stretched out, his fist grasping a strip of cloth.

"You are wise not to rejoice in your labors. This is all that is left of your kingdom," the prophet said, thrusting the ragged cloth into Solomon's hands. "Your servant, Jeroboam, possesses the rest of my torn garment, ten pieces, representing ten tribes of your kingdom. I delivered the message of the Lord to him this day, saying, 'I will tear the kingdom from the hand of Solomon and give ten tribes to you. But I will leave him one tribe for the sake of My servant David and for the sake of Jerusalem.' "

Solomon held the cloth tightly, his astonishment growing into anger as the prophet continued. "You forsook the Lord. You worshiped Ashtoreth, Chemosh, and Milcom, the god of the Ammonites. You have not followed His paths nor done what is right. You have not kept His laws or instructions as your father David did. The Lord has given one of your servants the kingdom. Two tribes will be left for your grandson, for the sake of David."

The prophet's eyes held Solomon's, as the message cut into Solomon's heart. He imagined all that he had worked for, all that he had created, all that gave him happiness, rent into pieces, tattered like the ragged cloth that lay in his hand.

As the prophet turned to leave, Solomon cried with fear, then rage, as his mind began to grasp the threatening situation. He quickly began to shout orders. He wanted someone to go after Jeroboam, now, to kill him. He tried to drown out the words of the prophet with action and fought to stop Jeroboam's uprising before it could sweep the nation and destroy his kingdom forever.

In the months to follow, Hadad and his band of robbers continued to torment Solomon, harassing the kingdom. Jeroboam, his own servant, took the prophet's words to heart and began stirring up the people and attempting to sway their allegiance—until Solomon's murderous rage drove him out of the land. Solomon watched his glorious kingdom fade from the shining city on a hill to a tarnished, sin-diseased shell, battered by unrest and turmoil.

His only escape was to retreat into his chambers, where he wrote and wrote, penning the secrets of his heart, his words of despair and confusion, his cries of vanity, over and over ...

He wrote about the Shulamite girl, escaping into memories of his young love. He confessed his failures and lamented the inevitability of death.

"The race is not to the swift, nor the battle to the strong," he wrote, "nor the bread to the wise, nor riches to men of understanding, but time and chance happen to them all, like fish taken in a cruel net and like birds caught in a snare."

The bitterness spewed onto the pages; he opened his soul and bared his faithless heart for all posterity to see. When he dreamt of the days in the garden, he wept over his loss of purity and love. "Remember your Creator in the days of your youth," he pleaded with his future readers, "While the sun and the light of the moon and the stars are not darkened ... remember your Creator."

Solomon felt the light darkening, and finally, when his passions were spent through the words he had written, he penned his final conclusions:

"Fear God and keep His commandments, for this is the whole duty of man. For God will bring every work into judgment, including every secret thing, whether it is good or whether it is evil."

Finally, one day he laid his pen down and smiled in relief. It seemed quiet. The thundering voice of the prophets, the turmoil of a nation lurching toward civil war, even the din of the false gods who vied for his heart and soul—all of it became a silent, mimed background to the peace that flooded his soul.

Wisdom, truth, and love had captured his heart again.[38]

§

DARK NIGHT OF THE SOUL

A curious monument stands in the Saratoga National Historical Park in New York. Its inscription reads: "In memory of the most brilliant soldier of the Continental Army, who was desperately wounded on this spot ... winning for his countrymen the decisive battle of the American Revolution and for himself the rank of major general." The monument doesn't reveal the man's name, but we know that historians describe Benedict Arnold as a once-brave hero, considered second only to George Washington.

But something went terribly wrong in the life of Benedict Arnold. He became disillusioned with his fight for freedom, and sold out to the enemy. Branded a traitor, he fled his country and died in disgrace in a faraway land. So deep was his regret and sorrow that he asked to be buried in his American uniform.[39]

In researching Solomon's life, I came across one line that has haunted me throughout the writing of this book and which I have referenced in a previous chapter. Josephus, the ancient Jewish historian, pronounced his final epitaph on Solomon's life saying, "And so, he died ingloriously."

Josephus saw Solomon just as the early Americans saw Benedict Arnold: a once brilliant and glorious life come to ruin, ending pathetically and tragically.

But the Solomon I've met through the Scriptures is quite different. Surrounded by the monuments to his success, I believe he saw this "inglorious end" looming ahead. He may have wanted to believe that his riches were still the outward signs of God's blessings, but like Benedict Arnold donning the American uniform one last time, I think he knew that his wealthy trappings had become a shabby symbol of the sorrow and emptiness within. As he began writing the personal confessions, the poetry, and the philosophy that became the book of *Ecclesiastes*, Solomon was at last ready to deal with the truth. A great discovery awaited him.

The king had entered what St. John of the Cross, a fifteenth century priest and poet, once described as the "dark night of the soul"—that time in one's life when the struggle to climb out of depression appears to be in vain.

Ecclesiastes is Solomon's confession of failure—and his triumph over despair. He understood now that the earthly desires men cherish are mere shadows of reality and truth. Even the great chase for the prizes of life and the pursuit of happiness eventually becomes an empty illusion.

Solomon portrays the endless cycle of futility that plagues each generation, doomed by nature to wear itself out in the pursuit of this unattainable happiness. No matter how much we rationalize, philosophize, or improve the means of our pursuit, the result is always the same: *"Vanity of vanities,"* Solomon cried. *"All is vanity."* All of it. Work, wisdom, righteousness, wealth, prestige, power, pleasure, even youth and vigor. It's all smoke and vapor, a passing wind.

Have you ever thought these thoughts? Have you feared that your life, no matter how hard you work and how much you succeed, will produce nothing of lasting value or fulfillment? "What hope is there," you might ask, "if a man like Solomon can be written off by a prominent historian as someone who died 'ingloriously'?" If you were to imagine yourself approaching the end of your life, would you be doing what you're doing now? Can you empathize with Benedict Arnold, longing one last time to put on the garments that represented a time of high ideals and commitment to goodness and truth? It's a terrible prospect to think of growing old with regrets.

If you have ever felt this sense of futility, if your heart aches with spiritual sorrow, welcome to the dark night of the soul.

You are in the very place Solomon found himself. In spite of *Ecclesiastes'* pessimistic and cynical tone, it's actually an honest exploration of truth and reality. The truth Solomon presents is not always pretty, but it is tempered by love, and more importantly, inspired by the Holy Spirit.

I see a man who is seeing his life clearly, perhaps for the first time. From the vantage point of old age, he recognizes his failures, and laments his shortcomings. Drawing on a storehouse of wisdom, he gradually directs us, then compels us, to surrender to the truth that will set us free.

But first, we must enter the darkness, where God's passion will take us, woo us, love us, hold us close to Him, and get us through the night.

Moses drew near the thick darkness where God was.

—Exodus 20:21

The people were afraid. They heard the thunder, witnessed the lightening and the smoking mountain, and trembled as they kept their distance. But Moses, the friend of God, moved closer. God had first appeared to him in the fiery light of a burning bush, and later in a cloud. Now, as he descended from Mount Sinai with the Ten Commandments, and saw the fear of his people, he knew he had to approach the unapproachable. He knew God waited in the thick darkness shrouding the mountain.

"All this signifies that our passage from false and errant notions of God is a passage from darkness to light,"[40] says Thomas Merton, writing of Moses' experience. Everything we see in this world as light is darkness, compared with the presence of God. The light in which God dwells might as well be dark, so blinding and unapproachable is it to us. In order for us to "see" God, to know His presence, and to commune with Him, we must pass through the "dark night of the soul," dying to this world, and to ourselves. Only then can we be born again and awaken to the spiritual world.

St. John of the Cross divides "night" into three stages, a parallel to nighttime: "These three parts of the night are all one night; but like night itself, it has three parts."[41] The first part, *senses*, is comparable to dusk, the point at which things begin to fade from sight. The second part, *faith*, is comparable to midnight, or total darkness. And the third part, *God*, is like dawn, the part which is nearest to the light of day.

DUSK

SENSES

Solomon's first personal encounter with the Lord occurred at night.

Remember that day of sacrifice at Gibeon? Afterward he fell into bed, exhausted, and allowed the world to fade away. He needed the Lord, as he wrestled with his future, and prayed a childlike prayer for help.

Solomon began his journey with the Lord, like so many of us, with a tender heart, eager and willing to receive God's gifts. I remember that moment in my own life, and how I looked at the world through new eyes. What a beautiful world I saw! So much to be enjoyed, so much to learn. Solomon was lavished with gifts, blessings, and honor from the Lord. All five of his senses were fed, delighted, and fulfilled.

The subtle deception began when Solomon began to fall in love with the world rather than the Creator of the world. He fell in love with the gifts rather than remaining in love with the Giver. He turned his eyes and heart away from the love of God in heaven to the love of everything under heaven. He stopped wanting what God wanted, and turned to his own lusts. Whatever his eyes could see, he desired. Wherever his tastes took him, he gladly followed. Whatever he wanted, he indulged in. He never denied himself, and eventually he replaced his love for the Lord with a love for himself.

Of course, not everything he did was bad. He immersed himself in philosophy and the study of human nature, and although he lived over three thousand years ago, his insights and knowledge are as keen as anything written today. But even that left him dissatisfied. Putting an intellectual face on self-indulgence doesn't stop the hidden erosion of the soul. He wrote, *"I devoted myself to study and to explore by wisdom all that is done under heaven. What a heavy burden God has laid on men! I have seen all the things that are done under the sun; all of them are meaningless, a chasing after the wind"* (Ecclesiastes 1:16–17 NIV).

And the dusk deepened, drawing him deeper into the night as he gave himself to the pursuit of pleasure. *"Come now, I will test you with pleasure,"* he wrote. *"So enjoy yourself"* (Ecclesiastes 2:1–2 NASU).

Solomon practiced the philosophy that says, "I should be able to do anything I want as long as it doesn't hurt anyone else." That may sound right, but as Solomon discovered, it doesn't hold true. It didn't work then any better than it works today. Solomon nearly destroyed a whole nation by indulging his lusts, and concluded in the end that, *"Behold, it too was futility"* (Ecclesiastes 2:1 NASU).

Did Solomon give up when sensual pleasure failed to satisfy? No! Did he realize that the night was closing in? Apparently not, for he relentlessly pursued satisfaction by throwing himself into work, constructing monuments to his ego, determined to build a legacy for future generations. Again, in his own words:

> I undertook great projects: I built houses for myself and planted vineyards. I made gardens and parks and planted all kinds of fruit trees in them. I made reservoirs to water groves of flourishing trees. I bought male and female slaves and had other slaves who were born in my house. I also owned more herds and flocks than anyone in Jerusalem before me. I amassed silver and gold for myself, and the treasure of kings and provinces. I acquired men and women singers, and a harem as well—the delights of the heart of man. I became greater by far than anyone in Jerusalem before me. In all this my wisdom stayed with me.
>
> I denied myself nothing my eyes desired; I refused my heart no pleasure. My heart took delight in all my work, and this was the reward for all my labor. Yet when I surveyed all that my hands had done and what I had toiled to achieve, everything was meaningless, a chasing after the wind; nothing was gained under the sun.
>
> —Ecclesiastes 2:4–11 NIV

The more Solomon sought to find satisfaction through his senses, *the more dull they became.* Slowly, subtly, Solomon entered into stage one of the dark night of the soul. Sin has its pleasure for a season, but then the season ends. Long shadows begin to obscure the vision and nothing looks bright or pretty anymore. There is nothing so miserable as a sinner who no longer enjoys his or her sin. But dusk doesn't last long. It deepens to the darkness of midnight.

MIDNIGHT

FAITH

There is something appealing about the dark. It conceals things we don't want to see. It also hides things we take for granted during the light of day. The wonderful thing about midnight, the darkest part of night, is that it makes you appreciate what little light there is.

St. John of the Cross likened midnight to faith. That might seem confusing, until you think about the Bible's definition of faith: *"The substance of things hoped for, the evidence of things not seen"* (Hebrews 11:1). The things we don't see are often the things of God. Areas in our lives where He is working, unknown to us. Prayers that are being answered in ways we don't understand, but by faith, in that darkest hour when *all* is dark, we learn to trust and to turn to the only source of light that is real. Jesus said, *"I am the light of the world"* (John 8:12). And then John assures us that *"In Him was life, and the life was the light of men"* (1:4).

When will the light of Jesus shine brighter than when it shines into the darkest midnight of your life? Midnight is the season that deepens our faith.

The Solomon who wrote the book of *Ecclesiastes* is a far different man than the idealist and poet who wrote the *Song of Solomon*. He is different from the practical, wise king who penned the *Proverbs*. The

Solomon of *Ecclesiastes* resides in the darkest hour of his life. The poetry is still there, but it burns with cynicism and bitterness. It is tainted by fatalism, and a "nothing matters" attitude. As the book progresses, a haunting beauty speaks to our hearts, as we recognize a change—subtle like the change of seasons—from bitter fatalism to a surrender of the will. He resigns himself to his fate—not a random fate, but a fate that is determined and designed. The same fate awaits us, with the discovery that even in the darkness we are never alone.

As you read the following passage, think of Solomon, writing with the soul of a poet, and exposing his heart to all of posterity:

To everything there is a season, a time for every purpose under heaven:

A time to be born, and a time to die; a time to plant, and a time to pluck what is planted;

A time to kill, and a time to heal; a time to break down, and a time to build up;

A time to weep, and a time to laugh; a time to mourn, and a time to dance;

A time to cast away stones, and a time to gather stones; a time to embrace, and a time to refrain from embracing;

A time to gain, and a time to lose; a time to keep, and a time to throw away;

A time to tear, and a time to sew; a time to keep silence, and a time to speak;

A time to love, and a time to hate; a time of war, and a time of peace.

—Ecclesiastes 3:1–8

Many centuries later, another poet and philosopher wrestled with many of these same issues. He also happens to be one of my favorite writers—Aurelius Augustine.

Sherwood Wirt says of Augustine, "He has been called the greatest African who ever lived, the keenest mind of the ancient world after Plato and Aristotle, the outstanding genius of the Roman Catholic Church and the spearhead of the Protestant Reformation."[42]

Born in A.D. 354, the son of a poor, pagan freeman and a devout Christian mother, Augustine was unusually intelligent and full of potential. Shoving aside his mother's prayers, he spent his adolescence staying out late, exploring sexual pleasure, and running with a rebellious gang. Said Augustine, "I was ashamed to be less scandalous than my peers."[43]

Nothing much has changed, has it?

Augustine continued a very "modern" and enlightened lifestyle into early adulthood. Higher education, political ambition, and respect as a scholar and teacher made him important. A mistress kept him company, and his very worldly, metropolitan lifestyle appeared satisfying to his peers.

But a spiritual struggle disquieted his soul. His years as a teacher frequently brought him into contact with Christian scholars. "Christ was for him a sentimental figure," Sherwood writes, "venerated by his mother but ignored by the philosophers he admired ... thus began a life-and-death struggle in the soul of the young African rhetor."[44]

Eventually, Augustine became intellectually convinced of Christianity's validity, but, "A chief difficulty was that his sensual desires continued unabated ... should he become a Christian, he knew he had to solve the problem of his carnality."[45]

Augustine was being driven toward midnight.

Like Solomon, Augustine possessed a great intellect, a curious mind, and a hearty sensual appetite. Their five senses were finely tuned and both men relished in their natural gifts. But like so many of us, they lacked one huge element in their lives.

We can see, hear, taste, touch, feel, and even smell our way through life. But when we long for spiritual fulfillment, none of these senses help. (For *"God is Spirit, and those who worship Him must worship in spirit and truth,"* Jesus said in John 4:23.)

When we are stumbling through the dark, yearning to see God, despairing of ever finding our way, that's when God reveals another "sense"—a glorious one that brings the experience and substance of heaven into our lives. Consider *faith* as a "spiritual sense." By faith we can "see" heavenly realities, we can "hear" the whisper of God speaking to our souls. We can experience the "love" of God shed abroad in our hearts, take in the sweet fragrance of the Lord, and "taste" and see how good the Lord is! The source of our faith is the Word of God, for *"faith comes by hearing, and hearing by the word of God"* (Romans 10:17).

Solomon had never stopped believing in God, but he lost his passion for God by expending it on sensual experiences. He left a banqueting table laden with satisfaction and settled for leftovers. Augustine, struggling to reach that table for the first time, got bogged down and worn out by the chains of sin.

Both men had to learn that when our energy is dissipated through pleasure, the pleasure becomes a bondage rather than a gift. Walking by faith, however, fulfills every passion, need, and even the desires that stir our souls.

DAWN

GOD

In the summer of A.D. 386, Augustine found many of his philosophical leanings deeply unsatisfying. His mistress was gone, his father had committed his life to Christ before he died, his mother was still praying for him, and the ground seemed to be crumbling beneath his feet. In despair, his soul swamped in darkness, he entered a friend's garden one day, threw himself under a tree, and wept. Shortly afterward, he was moved to pick up a copy of Paul's letter to the Romans, which happened to be sitting nearby, and began to read.

In the midst of Augustine's darkness, the light of love and truth came pouring in. He heard the knock upon his heart, and finally opened the door.

Later he would write, "I love you Lord, not doubtingly, but with absolute certainty. Your Word beat upon my heart until I fell in love with you, and now the universe and everything in it tells me to love you, and tells the same thing to all of us, so that we are without excuse."[46]

Dawn had broken in the life of Augustine.

What about our friend Solomon? Can you read the book of *Ecclesiastes* and see the dawn breaking in the midst of his dark cynicism and weary soul?

The answer of course is "Yes." I say of course because I believe, without doubt, that God will never abandon His children. When He allows us to walk through the dark, or even the valley of the shadow of death, He is teaching us to walk by faith. And He always takes us to the dawn. Whatever it takes to get us there, whatever we need to learn, Resurrection *always* follows Good Friday for those who believe.

I believe that Solomon is the prodigal son of the Old Testament. He was raised with love and blessings, but took his spiritual inheritance and went to a far country, far away from the intimate relationship with the Lord of his youth. One day, in the darkness of the life he had chosen, mired in the mud of the world he had created, he saw the light beckoning him home.

"Remember now your Creator in the days of your youth, before the difficult days come," he wrote. Later he repeated, *"Remember your Creator before the silver cord is loosed. ..."* (Ecclesiastes 12:1,6).

Finally, as the dawn broke, Solomon came home to the Lord, ending his literary confessions with this simple, understated conclusion:

> Let us hear the conclusion of the whole matter: Fear God, and keep his commandments: for this is the whole duty of man.
>
> —Ecclesiastes 12:13 KJV

I CAME TO LOVE YOU LATE

I think Solomon and Augustine would have enjoyed each other's company. In fact, they probably do! Solomon came home to the Lord late in life, and if he had been a contemporary of Augustine's, I believe he would have echoed the beautiful words Augustine penned in his own *Confessions*:

> I came to love you late, O Beauty so ancient and so new; I came to love you late. You were within me and I was outside, where I rushed about wildly searching for you like a monster loose in your beautiful world. You were with me but I was not with you. You called me, you shouted to me, you broke past my deafness. You bathed me in your light, you wrapped me in your splendor, you sent my blindness reeling. You gave out such a delightful

fragrance, and I drew it in and came breathing hard after you. I tasted, and it made me hunger and thirst; you touched me, and I burned to know your peace.[47]

Augustine's conversion is a passionate revelation of God's pursuing love. "You called me, you shouted to me, you broke past my deafness," he confessed. If you are ever unsure of God's desire for you, look over your shoulder. Look around you. Listen. He is calling, shouting. He longs to wrap you in His splendor, bathe you in His light, love you and bless you.

In *Ecclesiastes*, we met a man who "burned to know" God's peace. I felt such a deep sense of gratitude and relief when I realized that Solomon did indeed find redemption and peace in the end.

I have to confess, it's hard to say goodbye to Solomon. There's only the epilogue left! The study of his life has enriched me—and I hope you as well. His passion, his honesty, and his wisdom have moved me. I pray that if you have read this far, you have also seen God move and have felt Him stirring your heart and rekindling a passion for Him and for life.

If you take nothing else away from this book, I pray that you will always remember the shepherd girl and her king. I hope you'll know that you can return to the love of God and realize that He promised to never leave you nor forsake you.

Remember, we are all like the shepherd girl; even when she felt unworthy, when her own passion waned and she grew weary of life, she knew she could come to the garden and be comforted and encouraged by the words that so beautifully reflect God's eternal passion for us:

> I am my beloved's and my beloved is mine. ... and his desire is toward me.
>
> —Song 6:3, 7:10

Epilogue
FIRST LOVE

TWILIGHT *began to settle over him like a warm blanket. Walking among the neat rows of vines and lush greenery, Solomon felt sheltered from old age and the turmoil of his kingdom.*

The vineyard had grown so tall and healthy this year that the plants rose above his tall frame. His magnificent hair, thinning near the top, was still full, but whiter and wispier than in years past.

A golden glow cast itself over the sky as the sun settled on the horizon. The dusky hue of the grapes began to blend into the walls of foliage, creating a tapestry of colors. The moisture glistening on the fruit sparkled like jewels. He heard the water racing over the rocks in the brook, singing its merry song, and walked over to it, amazed at its crystal clarity as it danced in the evening light that played through the trees.

He saw her standing on the other side of the stream. Her frock was whiter, her smile more beautiful, her countenance less timid. His beloved ... Wisdom ... love.

She held out her hand and beckoned him toward her. He felt strong again, like a young stag, and she like a pretty gazelle. He laughed as he ran after her, up to the mountain of spices.

*Together, they would reach the beautiful city on the hill ...
and remain there ... forever.*

——————————— § ———————————

Then Solomon rested with his fathers, and was buried in the
City of David his father.

—2 Chronicles 9:31

CONTACT INFORMATION

For teachings by Pastor Ray, for prayer, or for church information, please contact Maranatha Chapel:

10752 Coastwood Road
San Diego, CA 92127
858.613.7800
www.maranathachapel.org

NOTES

PROLOGUE: *THE SHEPHERD GIRL AND THE KING*

[1] Adapted from the Song of Solomon. Note: each section at the beginning of the chapters is an adaptation of the Scriptures, particularly Solomon's writings.

Chapter One: *BELOVED*

[2] Source unknown.

[3] Wirt, Sherwood. *Jesus Man of Joy* (Eugene, OR: Harvest House Publishers, Inc., 1999), p. 116.

[4] McGee, Vernon J. *Thru the Bible* (Nashville, TN: Thomas Nelson Publishers, 1982), Vol. III, p. 144.

[5] Spurgeon, C.H. (February 28, 1892). "Living, Loving, Lasting Union." *Metropolitan Tabernacle Pulpit*, online version. Retrieved October 30, 2003, from http://www.spurgeon.org/sermons/2245.htm.

Chapter Two: *CONSUMING PASSION*

[6] Psalms 57 and 61.

[7] Adapted from 1 Kings 2-3; 2 Chronicles 1; the account of this story as it appears in *The Life and Works of Flavius Josephus*, translated by William Whiston (Philadelphia, PA, and Toronto, OH: The John C. Winston Company, 1957), Book VIII; and Packer, J.I., Merrill Tenney, and William White. *The Bible Almanac* (Nashville, TN: Thomas Nelson Publishers, 1980).

[8] Tozer, A.W. taken from "Today God is First" by Os Hillman. Retrieved December 2, 2003, from http://www.crosswalk.com/faith/devotionals/marketplace/547360.html.

[9] Levy, Daniel S. (1999, January 19). "Requiems for Jackie." *Time Magazine.* Retrieved October 22, 2003, from http://www.time.com/time/archive/preview/from_search/0,10987,1101990118-18307,00.html.

[10] Guinness, Os. *The Call* (Nashville, TN: Word Publishing, 1998). p. 75.

[11] Ibid.

Chapter Three: *LOVE THAT WON'T LET GO*

[12] Adapted from 1 Kings 1–2 and the account of this story as it appears in *The Life and Works of Flavius Josephus*, Book VIII.

[13] Dorsett, Lyle W. *A Passion for Souls, The Life of D.L. Moody* (Chicago, IL: Moody Publishers, 1997), p. 192.

[14] Lewis, C.S. *The Four Loves* (New York: Harcourt Brace Jovanovich, 1960), p. 169.

Chapter Four: *THE ART OF LIVING*

[15] Adapted from Proverbs 7–9.

[16] Jenson, Ron. *Make a Life, Not Just a Living* (Nashville, TN: Thomas Nelson Publishers, 1995).

[17] McKinney, Michael. "Where is the Wisdom We Have Lost in Knowledge?" Retrieved October 31, 2003, from *Foundations Magazine*, online version: http://www.foundationsmag.com/wisdom.html.

[18] Wirt, Sherwood and Kersten Beckstrom (eds.). *Living Quotations for Christians* (London: Hodder & Stoughton, 1974), p. 93.

[19] Lewis, C.S. *The Lion, the Witch and the Wardrobe* (Hammersmith, London: Diamond Books, a division of HarperCollins Publishers, this edition 1999), p. 243.

[20] Delany, Sarah and Elizabeth. *The Delany Sisters' Book of Everyday Wisdom* (New York, NY: Kodansha America, Inc., 1994).

[21] Source unknown.

Chapter Five: *WHAT'S REAL?*

[22] Adapted from 1 Kings 3:16–28 and the account of this story as it appears in *The Life and Works of Flavius Josephus.*

[23] Sockman, Ralph W. *The Highway of God* (New York, NY: The Macmillan Company, 1942).

Chapter Six: *A DWELLING PLACE FOR GOD*

[24] Adapted from 1 Kings 5,6 and 2 Chronicles 2–7.

[25] Dostoevsky, Fyodor. *The Brothers Karamazov,* translated by Constance Garnett, Book V, Chapter 5. <http://www.ccel.org/d/dostoevsky/karamozov/karamozov.html>, October 28, 2003.

[26] O'Donnell, Maureen (September 16, 2003). "Born a Jew in War, Today a Priest." *Chicago Sun Times,* online edition. Retrieved October 30, 2003, from http://www.suntimes.com/output/religion/cst-nws-priest16.html.

[27] Source unknown.

[28] Guinness, Os. *The Call,* p. 29.

[29] Jenson, Ron. *Make a Life, Not Just a Living,* p. 78.

Chapter Seven: *KING OF THE WORLD!*

[30] Adapted from 1 Kings 9; 2 Chronicles 8 and the account of this story as it appears in *The Life and Works of Flavius Josephus,* Book VIII, Chapters V–VII.

[31] Yancey, Philip. *Where is God When it Hurts?* (Grand Rapids, MI: Zondervan, 1977), pp. 23–25.

[32] Stedman, Ray C. *The Christian and Worldliness.* Retrieved November 26,

2003, from http://www.pbc.org/dp/stedman/misc/worldly2.html.

[33] Guinness, Os. *The Call,* p. 140.

Chapter Eight: *THE QUEEN OF SHEBA AND OTHER FOREIGN WOMEN*

[34] Adapted from 1 Kings 10; 2 Chronicles 9; the account of this story as it appears in *The Life and Works of Flavius Josephus*, Book VIII, Chapter VI; and http://swagga.com/queen.htm#makeda.

[35] Clapp, Nicholas. *Sheba: Through the Desert in Search of the Legendary Queen* (Boston, MA: Houghton Mifflin Company, 2001), pp. 23–28,88,221.

[36] Frost, Robert. *Stopping by Woods on a Snowy Evening.*

[37] James, Joyce. *Dubliner* (New York, NY: The Modern Library, 1993), p. 35.

Chapter Nine: *A NIGHT OF PASSION*

[38] Sources: Ecclesiastes, 1 Kings 11, and *The Life and Works of Flavius Josephus.*

[39] Kennedy, Peter. *From Generation to Generation* (Uhrichsville, OH: Barbour Books, 1998).

[40] Merton, Thomas. *The Ascent to Truth* (San Diego, CA, and New York, NY: Harvest Books, Harcourt, Inc., 2002), p. 33.

[41] Peers, E. Allison, ed. *Dark Night of the Soul,* by St. John of the Cross (New York, NY: Image Books, 1959).

[42] Wirt, Sherwood. *Faith's Heroes* (Englewood, CO: Cornerstone Books, 1979), p. 29.

[43] Ibid, p. 31.

[44] Ibid, p. 34.

[45] Ibid, p. 35.

[46] Wirt, Sherwood, translator. *The Confessions of St. Augustine in Modern English* (Grand Rapids, MI: Zondervan Publishing, date unknown), p. 124.

[47] Ibid, p. 125.